ON THE WAY 1

Englisch für die Erwachsenenbildung

Arbeitsbuch

von
Joan Corliss Bartel und Gernot Häublein

in Zusammenarbeit mit
Dieter Kranz, Günter Reichwein und Geoff Tranter

unter Leitung und Mitwirkung
der Verlagsredaktion Weiterbildung Fremdsprachen

Ernst Klett Verlag

ON THE WAY 1 – Arbeitsbuch

von
Joan Corliss Bartel M.A., Fremdsprachenpädagogin in der Erwachsenenbildung, Cambridge, Mass.;
Gernot Häublein M.A., Englischlehrer an der Volkshochschule Landshut, freiberuflicher Redakteur und Autor

in Zusammenarbeit mit
Dr. Dieter Kranz M.A., Akademischer Oberrat an der Universität Münster und Englischlehrer an der Volkshochschule Münster;
Günter Reichwein, Fachbereichsleiter Sprachen an der Volkshochschule Duisburg;
Geoff Tranter, Fachbereichsleiter Sprachen an der Volkshochschule Dortmund, Landesprüfungsbeauftragter für das Volkshochschul-Zertifikat Englisch 1 in Nordrhein-Westfalen

unter Leitung und Mitwirkung
der Verlagsredaktion Weiterbildung Fremdsprachen;
Leiter: Wolfgang H. Kaul M.A.;
Mitarbeit an diesem Werk: Derrick Jenkins, Lutz Rohrmann, Verlagsredakteure.

Zeichnungen
Joachim Schreiber, Schwäbisch Gmünd.

ISBN 3-12-500150-1

1. Auflage   1 9 8 7 6 5 | 1990 89 88 87 86

Alle Drucke dieser Auflage können im Unterricht nebeneinander benutzt werden, sie sind untereinander unverändert. Die letzte Zahl bezeichnet das Jahr dieses Druckes.
© Ernst Klett Verlage GmbH u. Co. KG, Stuttgart 1981. Alle Rechte vorbehalten.
Druck: Ludwig Auer, Donauwörth. Printed in Germany.

Inhalt

Unit 1	Übungen	8		**Unit 8**	Übungen	68
	Grammatik	11			Grammatik	74
Unit 2	Übungen	12		**Unit 9**	Übungen	77
	Grammatik	18			Grammatik	88
Unit 3	Übungen	20		**Unit 10**	Übungen	90
	Grammatik	28			Grammatik	98
Unit 4	Übungen	31		**Unit 11**	Übungen	100
	Grammatik	38			Grammatik	106
Unit 5	Übungen	39		**Unit 12**	Übungen	108
	Grammatik	48			Grammatik	118
Unit 6	Übungen	50		**Unit 13**	Übungen	120
	Grammatik	56			Grammatik	127
Unit 7	Übungen	58		**Unit 14**	Übungen	128
	Grammatik	66			Grammatik	135

Tips für die Arbeit mit diesem Buch	4		**Schlüssel**	137
Phonetic alphabet	7		**Hörtexte**	149

Tips für die Arbeit mit diesem Buch

Die Aufgaben des Arbeitsbuchs

Dieses Buch ist in erster Linie für Sie als Lernende geschrieben: Sie können es zu Hause völlig selbständig – also auch ohne Lehrerhilfe – zum Wiederholen und Vertiefen des im Kursunterricht Gelernten benutzen. Deswegen sind alle Übungen und die sonstigen Teile dieses Buches auf deutsch erklärt. Und es gibt zu jeder Aufgabe nur **eine** oder eine **begrenzte Zahl** richtiger Lösungen; diese sind sämtlich im Schlüssel am Ende des Buches angegeben. Damit können Sie nach jeder Übung selbst kontrollieren, ob Sie eine sprachliche Schwierigkeit schon sicher beherrschen oder noch weiterüben sollten.

Auch wenn Sie einmal eine Unterrichtsstunde versäumt haben, kann Ihnen das *Arbeitsbuch* – zusammen mit dem *Lehrbuch* und den *Cassetten* – helfen, die entstandene ‚Lücke' zu überbrücken.

Inhalt und Aufbau des Arbeitsbuchs

Im Mittelpunkt des Kursunterrichts steht das **Sprechen**. Mit Hilfe des *Arbeitsbuchs* üben Sie zu Hause verstärkt das **Schreiben, Lesen** und **Hören** englischer Texte bzw. Gespräche. Alle diese Übungen werden Sie schriftlich bearbeiten: Deshalb ist im *Arbeitsbuch* genügend Platz zum Schreiben in Form von Leerzeilen eingeplant. Hier gleich ein Praxistip: Benutzen Sie immer einen weichen Bleistift; so können Sie unrichtige Lösungen ohne Mühe ausradieren und erneut ins Buch schreiben.

Zu den *Lehrbuch*-Units 1–14 gibt es je eine *Arbeitsbuch*-Unit mit Übungen und einer Grammatik-Zusammenfassung.

Die einzelnen Übungen sind in der Regel so aufgebaut wie das folgende Beispiel aus Unit 1:

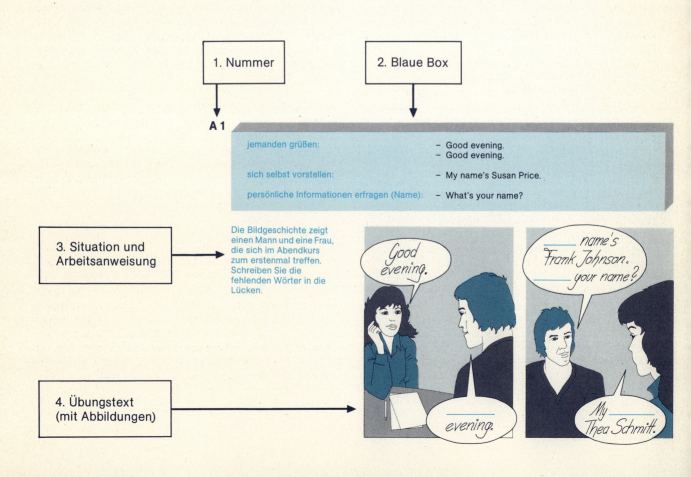

Tips für die Arbeit mit diesem Buch

1. Nummer

A 1 bedeutet: Diese Übung können Sie zu Hause bearbeiten, sobald im Unterricht der *Lehrbuch*-Schritt **A 1** durchgenommen ist.

A 1
↓
A 3 bedeutet: Diese Übung erst nach Durchnahme der *Lehrbuch*-Schritte **A 1, A 2** und **A 3** bearbeiten. Hier wird Stoff aus diesen drei Schritten geübt.

2. Blaue Box:
Hier wird vor jeder Übung knapp zusammengefaßt, was Sie in den entsprechenden *Lehrbuch*-Schritten neu gelernt haben: „Sprechabsichten" (linke Spalte), die Sie mit Hilfe bestimmter sprachlicher Mittel nun ausdrücken können.

3. Deutsche Situationsbeschreibung/Arbeitsanweisung:
Hier wird die Situation beschrieben und gesagt, wie Sie die Übung machen sollen.

4. Übungs- und Auswertungstext (mit Abbildungen):
Zumeist gelenkt oder unterstützt durch Zeichnungen, Fotos und realistisch wiedergegebene Ausschnitte aus Zeitungen, Prospekten usw. wiederholen und festigen Sie hier das im Unterricht neu eingeführte Sprachmaterial. Häufig wenden Sie es auch gleich in anderen Situationen oder Textarten an als im *Lehrbuch*. Das ist notwendig, damit Sie später Ihre Englischkenntnisse „in allen Lebenslagen" gebrauchen können.

Hörverständnisübungen/Cassette zum Arbeitsbuch

Mit Hilfe dieser Übungen können Sie lernen, z. B. aus einem Gespräch oder einer Lautsprecheransage die für Sie wichtige Information herauszuhören.
Zu diesem Zweck haben wir eine eigene Compact-Cassette entwickelt (Klettnummer 50016).

Diese Compact-Cassette enthält 19 Übungen zum Hörverständnis. Im Arbeitsbuch sind diese Übungen mit dem Symbol für Hörverständnisübungen gekennzeichnet. Arbeiten Sie bitte in folgenden Schritten:

- Lesen Sie zuerst die **Arbeitsanweisung** zur Übung im Arbeitsbuch.
- Hören Sie dann den englischen **Text** der Übung auf der Cassette. Versuchen Sie zunächst nur, diesen Text in groben Zügen zu verstehen.
- Konzentrieren Sie sich ganz aufs Hören. Lesen Sie bitte nicht mit.
- Sobald Sie das akustische Signal hören, schalten Sie bitte Ihr Gerät ab. Lesen Sie nun die **Aufgaben** im Arbeitsbuch durch. Versuchen Sie aber noch nicht, sie zu lösen.
- Spulen Sie die Cassette zum Anfang der Übung zurück (das Bandzählwerk hilft dabei) und hören Sie den ganzen Text zum zweitenmal. Jetzt konzentrieren Sie sich auf die gesuchten Informationen.
- Versuchen Sie nun, die im Arbeitsbuch gestellten Aufgaben zu lösen. Hören Sie dazu – wenn nötig – die Cassette sooft Sie wollen.

Zur Kontrolle, ob Sie alle Aufgaben richtig gelöst haben, gibt es neben dem Schlüssel auch die gesammelten ‚Hörtexte' im Buchanhang. Schauen Sie diese aber bitte erst dann an, wenn Sie die Aufgaben gelöst haben. Wenn Sie die Cassette nach dem letzten Abhören nicht zurückspulen, steht sie an der richtigen Stelle für die nächste Übung.

Die Hörverständnisübungen beginnen mit Unit 2, Übung B 1 ➔ B 2.

Außerdem enthält die Cassette Texte zur Lösungskontrolle für einige Aussprachenübungen. Diese sind im Arbeitsbuch nur mit dem Cassettensymbol gekennzeichnet.

Der Schlüssel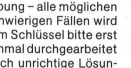

Am Ende des Buches finden Sie – unter der gleichen Nummer wie die entsprechende Übung – alle möglichen Lösungen zu jeder Aufgabe; in schwierigen Fällen wird erklärt und begründet. Sehen Sie im Schlüssel bitte erst nach, wenn Sie die ganze Übung einmal durchgearbeitet haben. Korrigieren Sie nicht einfach unrichtige Lösungen, sondern machen Sie die ganze Übung noch einmal durch, sobald Sie sich über Ihre „Fehler" im klaren sind. Dabei hilft die Grammatik-Zusammenfassung.

Tips für die Arbeit mit diesem Buch

Die Grammatik-Zusammenfassungen (Grammar)

Mit jeder Unit des Lehrbuchs lernen Sie auch mehr vom System der englischen Sprache kennen. Das heißt, Sie erfahren, wie Wörter, Wendungen und Sätze richtig aufgebaut und wie sie in bestimmten Situationen angemessen verwendet werden.

Die Grammatik-Zusammenfassung im *Arbeitsbuch* sammelt zu jeder Unit die wichtigsten neuen Wortformen und Satzstrukturen und ordnet sie in den Zusammenhang mit schon Bekanntem ein. Oft werden Aufbau und Verwendung einer sprachlichen Struktur zusätzlich in knappen Erläuterungssätzen bewußtgemacht. Dies besonders dann, wenn wichtige Unterschiede zwischen dem Englischen und dem Deutschen vorliegen, die erfahrungsgemäß besondere Lernschwierigkeiten auslösen. Auf solche tückischen Fehlerquellen wird durch das Zeichen ❗ aufmerksam gemacht.

Wenn Sie beim Üben mit dem *Arbeitsbuch* auf eine Schwierigkeit stoßen, wenn Ihnen eine Wortform oder eine Satzstruktur unklar ist, sehen Sie bitte in der Grammatik-Zusammenfassung nach. Dort werden Sie in der Regel ausreichend Information zu Ihrem Problem finden, oft auch Rückverweise auf frühere Units, wo ähnliche Probleme schon einmal behandelt wurden.
Beispiel: ➔ Unit 3.7 – bedeutet, daß Sie in der Grammatik-Zusammenfassung zu Unit 3 unter Punkt 7 weitere Hinweise finden können.

Diese begleitende Grammatik hilft Ihnen also vor allem bei der Nachbereitung des Kursunterrichts und beim Lösen der Übungen im Arbeitsbuch. Daneben können Sie sich mit ihrer Hilfe auch einmal im Überblick des gelernten Grammatikstoffs vergewissern, bevor Sie zur nächsten Unit weitergehen.

Wieviel häusliche Arbeit und wann?

Weil das Englischlernen ohne wiederholendes und vertiefendes Üben zwischen den Unterrichtsstunden selten oder nie zum Erfolg führt, gibt es dieses *Arbeitsbuch* mit *Compact-Cassette* zu ON THE WAY 1. Für Ihre Lernarbeit zu Hause (oder in Arbeitspausen usw.) sollten Sie etwa genauso viel Zeit wie für den Kursunterricht einsetzen.

Ein Praxistip zum Schluß: Lernen Sie möglichst an jedem unterrichtsfreien Tag mit *Arbeitsbuch* und *Cassette* 20–30 Minuten, nicht an einem Tag 2 oder 3 Stunden auf einmal.

Autoren und Verlagsredaktion

Symbole	📼	= Einsatz der Cassette
	👂	= Hörverständnisübung

Quellennachweis
Fotos: Anthony Verlag, Starnberg (© H. Bergmann): 131 (4); Bavaria, Gauting: 131 (1); BBC Modern English, London: 17; Blackpool Corporation: 85; Colorific, London: 131 (5); dpa, Frankfurt: 20 *(a, d)*; 39 *(b, d)*; Image Bank (H. Wendler): 39 *(c)*; Laenderpress, Düsseldorf: 131 (3); Mauritius, Mittenwald: 20 *(c)*; Sheldon Mittelman, MCA Inc. (courtesy of Universal Pictures): 70; Picturepoint, London: 39 *(a)*; Rapho, Paris: 20 *(b)*; Lutz Rohrmann, Mannheim: 132 (1–2); Wilhelm Rohrmann, Heidelberg: 20 *(e)*; Clive Sawyer, Crawley, Sussex: 14 (8); 15 (1–4); 23; 37; 43; 51 (1–3); 53 (1–4); 59 (1–5); 77 (1–3); 78; 79 (1–6); 131 (2); Harald Stetzer, Schwäbisch Gmünd: 13 (1–2); 14 (1–7);

Cartoons: Mirror Group Newspapers, London: 129; Oxford University Press, Oxford: 89; Punch Publications Ltd, London: 49; 85; 153;
Zeichnungen: Harald Stetzer, Schwäbisch Gmünd: 64 (2); 103 (1–7);
Piktogramme: ERCO Leuchten, Lüdenscheid (© 1976 by ERCO Leuchten GmbH): 27; 97;
Realien: Godfrey Davis (Car Hire) Ltd, Bushey, Watford: 93.

Alle übrigen Zeichnungen, Karten und Pläne sind von Joachim Schreiber, Schwäbisch Gmünd.

Phonetic alphabet Lautschrift

[:] bedeutet, daß der vorangehende Laut lang ist
['] bedeutet, daß die folgende Silbe eine Hauptbetonung erhält
[ˌ] bedeutet, daß die folgende Silbe eine Nebenbetonung erhält

[i:]	meet [mi:t]		[p]	pub [pʌb]
[ɑ:]	father ['fɑ:ðə]		[b]	bye [baɪ]
[ɔ:]	daughter ['dɔ:tə]		[t]	teacher ['ti:tʃə]
[u:]	school [sku:l]		[d]	daughter ['dɔ:tə]
[ɜ:]	firm [fɜ:m]		[k]	clerk [klɑ:k]
			[g]	good [gʊd]
[ɔ̃:]	restaurant ['restərɔ̃:ŋ]		[tʃ]	teacher ['ti:tʃə]
			[dʒ]	job [dʒɒb]
[ɪ]	in [ɪn]		[f]	firm [fɜ:m]
[e]	yes [jes]		[v]	evening ['i:vnɪŋ]
[æ]	thanks [θæŋks]		[θ]	thanks [θæŋks]
[ʌ]	son [sʌn]		[ð]	this [ðɪs]
[ɒ]	job [dʒɒb]		[s]	son [sʌn]
[ʊ]	good [gʊd]		[z]	is [ɪz]
[ə]	father ['fɑ:ðə]		[ʃ]	she [ʃi:]
			[ʒ]	television ['telɪˌvɪʒn]
[eɪ]	name [neɪm]		[h]	he [hi:]
[aɪ]	my [maɪ]		[m]	my [maɪ]
[ɔɪ]	toilet ['tɔɪlɪt]		[n]	now [naʊ]
[əʊ]	show [ʃəʊ]		[ŋ]	evening ['i:vnɪŋ]
[aʊ]	now [naʊ]		[l]	like [laɪk]
[ɪə]	here [hɪə]		[r]	room [ru:m]
[eə]	where [weə]		[w]	where [weə]
[ʊə]	tourist ['tʊərɪst]		[j]	yes [jes]

1 Unit

eight 8

A 1

jemanden grüßen:	– Good evening. – Good evening.
sich selbst vorstellen:	– My name's Susan Price.
persönliche Informationen erfragen (Name):	– What's your name?

Die Bildgeschichte zeigt einen Mann und eine Frau, die sich im Abendkurs zum erstenmal treffen. Schreiben Sie die fehlenden Wörter in die Lücken.

A 2

sich selbst vorstellen:	– I'm Susan Price…
jemanden vorstellen:	– and this is Doris Krüger.

Sie stellen sich und Ihre Bekannte einem jungen Kanadier vor, mit dem Sie auf einem Fest ins Gespräch kommen. Ergänzen Sie schriftlich:

Sie: I'm _Eva Rösner_ and _this_ is _Monika Kolb_.

Kanadier: _Good_ evening.

Bekannte: _Good evening_.

Sie: And _what's your_ name?

Kanadier: _My name's_ Paul Wright.
I'm

Unit 1

A 3

persönliche Informationen erfragen und geben (Herkunft):
– Where are you from?
– I'm from Essen.
– I'm from Essen, too.

In einem Touristenlokal Ihrer Heimatstadt kommen Sie und ein Freund mit einer Amerikanerin ins Gespräch.
Ergänzen Sie schriftlich:

Schreiben Sie nun das ganze Gespräch auf, um die englische Rechtschreibung zu üben.

Judy: Good evening, I'm Judy Brown
Sie: Good evening, my name's Eva Rösner
Freund: And I'm Dieter Kühn
Judy: I'm from New York. And where are you from
Sie: I'm from Nürnberg
Freund: And I'm from Nürnberg too

Unit 1

A 4 → A 5

persönliche Informationen erfragen und geben (Herkunft):
- Where's he from?/Where's she from?
- He's from Frankfurt./She's from Salzburg.

sich verabschieden:
- Goodbye!

1. Sie sind mit einer Reisegruppe soeben in Ihrem Londoner Hotel eingetroffen. An der Bar möchte ein freundlicher Gast Sie kennenlernen. Sie sprechen als einziger etwas Englisch. Ergänzen Sie schriftlich:

Gast: Good evening. My _name's_ Ellis Miller.
Sie: _Good evening_. I'm _Eva Rösner_ I'm from _Nürnberg_.
This _is_ Frau Nissen.
Gast: Where's _she_ from?
Sie: She's _from_ Bremen.
And _this_ is Herr Kluve.
Gast: _Where are you_ from?
Sie: _I'm_ from Bremen, _too_.
This _is_ Frl. Braun; _She's from_ Salzburg.
And Herr Bertschi's _from_ Berne.

2. Where's she from?
Where's he from?

a	Judy Brown	Bremen
b	Frau Nissen →	Berne
c	Herr Kluve	Salzburg
d	Frl. Braun	New York
e	Herr Bertschi	

Sehen Sie in den Übungen **A 3** und **A 4→5** nach und schreiben Sie:

a _Judy Brown's from New York_
b _Frau Nissen's from Bremen._
c _Herr Kluve's from Bremen_
d _Frl. Braun's from Salzburg_
e _Herr Bertschi's from Berne_

Grammar Unit 1

1. Questions with question words: what?, where?
Fragen mit Fragewörtern

- **What**'s your name?
- My name's **Bernd Hansen**.

- Wie heißt du/heißen Sie?/Wie ist dein/Ihr Name?
- Ich heiße/Mein Name ist Bernd Hansen.

- **Where** are you **from**?
- I'm **from Essen**.

- Wo bist du/sind Sie her?
- Ich bin aus Essen.

2. Personal pronouns: I, you, he, she
Persönliche Fürwörter

- **I**'m Susan Price.
- Where are **you** from?

- This is **Doris Krüger**.
- Where's **she** from?

- This is **Gerd Seeger**.
- Where's **he** from?

I	ich
you	du/Sie
she	sie
he	er

3. Possessive pronouns: my, your
Besitzanzeigende Fürwörter

- **My** name's Susan Price.
- What's **your** name?

my **your**	mein(e) dein(e)/Ihr(e)

4. be: short forms and long forms   be (sein): Kurzformen und Langformen

short forms	long forms	
I'm	I am	from Essen.
	Where are	you from?
She's	She is	from Salzburg.
He's	He is	from Mülheim.
Where's	Where is	he from?
What's	What is	your name?
My name's	... name is	Gerd Seeger.

Kurzformen werden vor allem in der gesprochenen Sprache verwendet, zunehmend aber auch in persönlichen Schreiben (Postkarte, Brief).

❗ Von **are** gibt es in der Verbindung **where are** keine geschriebene Kurzform.

5. too   auch

I'm from Essen, **too**.	Ich bin auch aus Essen.

Im Gegensatz zu **auch** steht **too** am Satzende.

2 Unit

twelve 12

A 1

jemanden grüßen und auf einen Gruß reagieren:	– How do you do? My name's…
	– How do you do? I'm…
	– Nice to meet you.
	– Hello.
	– Hello.
	– How are you?
	– I'm fine. And you?
	– Not so bad.
sich bedanken:	– …, thanks.

Alan Mills gibt eine Party und hat verschiedene Geschäftsfreunde eingeladen. Schreiben Sie die Begrüßungsgespräche anhand der Bilder (links) nieder.

Alan: Hello, Richard.
Richard: Hello Alan.
Alan: How are you?
Richard: I'm fine.

Alan: Hello, Susan.
Susan: Hello, Alan.
Alan, this is Miss Jones from Leeds.
Alan: How do you do?
Miss Jones: How do you do?

Mike Rogers: How do you do? I'm Mike Rogers.
Thomas Price: How do you do, I'm Thomas Price.
Mike Rogers: Nice to meet you.

Unit 2

A 2

persönliche Informationen geben (Verwandtschaftsbeziehungen/Beruf): — This is my wife Jill. She's a housewife.

a This is his _father_. b This is _his mother_. This is Graham Owen. c And this is _his wife_.

d This is her _husband_. This is Jill Lennard. e This is _her daughter_. f And this is _her son_.

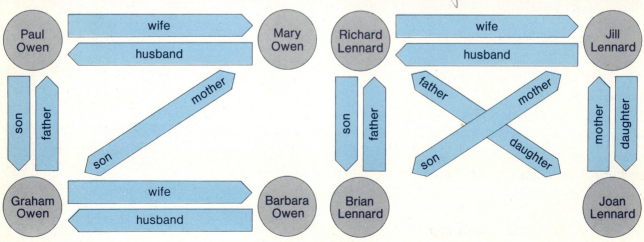

2 Unit

fourteen 14

A 2 → A 3

Are you a teacher?

Are you a shop-assistant?

Are you a housewife?

Are you an electrician?

Are you a clerk?

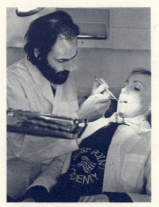
Are you a dentist?

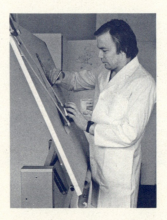
Are you an engineer?

No, I'm a waitress.

A 2 → A 4

persönliche Informationen erfragen und geben (Beruf):	– What's your job? – I'm a clerk.
persönliche Informationen erfragen und geben (Telefonnummer):	– What's your phone number? – It's 761 2409.

Unit 2

Frank Jones

Susan Jones

Richard Jones

Ann Jones

A 2 ↓ A 4

Der Quizmaster der 'Family Show' fragt seine Sekretärin, wer sich noch als Show-Teilnehmer beworben hat und notiert die Antworten.
Ergänzen Sie das Gespräch mit Hilfe der Bilder.

Secretary: The Jones family: Frank Jones …
Quizmaster: What's his job?
Secretary: He's _a teacher_.
Quizmaster: What's _his_ phone number?
Secretary: It's 733–2145.
And his wife Susan … _Jones_
Quizmaster: _What's her_ job?
Secretary: _She's a teacher, too_ , ____.
And his father and mother, Richard and Ann Jones.
Quizmaster: Richard … _Jones, what's his_ job?
Secretary: _he's an electrician_
Quizmaster: And Ann … _Jones_
Secretary: _She's a housewife_

Wortschatzübung: Die Zahlen

Verbinden Sie die Punkte 1–9 in der richtigen Reihenfolge. Was für eine Figur ergibt sich?

A 4

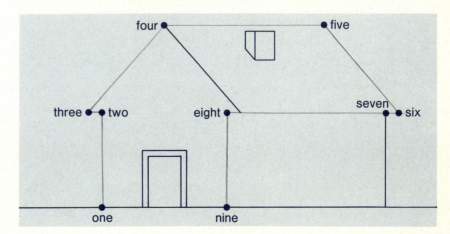

It's a _house_.

2 Unit

A 1 → B 1 Wortschatzübung

In den folgenden Wortgruppen findet sich immer ein Wort oder Ausdruck, das/der nicht zu den anderen paßt. Schreiben Sie das nicht passende Element in die Leerzeile.

a Hello./Good evening./Good morning./Goodbye.

Goodbye

b How do you do?/See you later./Goodbye./Bye.

How do you do

c daughter/mother/wife/husband

husband

d waitress/teacher/daughter/clerk

daughter

e father/Mr/husband/son

_Mr._

B 1 → B 2

Benutzen Sie die Compact-Cassette, um das folgende neue Telefonverzeichnis der Firma Johnson Export Ltd zu ergänzen.

Name	Job	Room	Phone
Clarke, Brenda			
Francis, Ann			
Harris, Simon			
Morrison, Alan			
Müller, Thomas			
Taylor, June			
Wilson, John			

17 seventeen Unit 2

B 3

In einem Pub spricht Sie ein Engländer an. Wählen Sie eine geeignete Antwort zu seinen Äußerungen.

1. *Engländer:* Good evening.
   Sie: a ☐ How do you do?
   b ☒ Good evening.
   c ☐ My name's …

2. *Engländer:* My name's Bill Jones. How do you do?
   Sie: a ☒ Fine, thanks, and you?
   b ☐ I'm …
   c ☒ How do you do? I'm …

3. *Engländer:* This is my wife Alice.
   Sie: a ☐ I'm …
   b ☐ Good morning.
   c ☒ Nice to meet you.

4. *Engländer:* Where are you from?
   Sie: a ☐ They're from Germany.
   b ☒ I'm from Germany.
   c ☐ He's from Germany.

5. *Engländer:* What about a drink?
   Sie: a ☒ Yes, thanks, a gin and tonic, please.
   b ☐ And you?
   c ☐ A gin and tonic.

Von den rechts aufgeführten Wortpaaren wird jeweils nur *ein* Wort zweimal vorgesprochen. Entscheiden Sie, welches gesprochen wurde, und unterstreichen Sie es.

a see – she
b we're – where
c his – he's
d her – here

e John – Joan
f no – now
g Miss – Mrs

B 4

Unit 2 Grammar

1. Questions with question words: how?
Fragen mit Fragewörtern

– **How** are you?	– Wie geht's?
– I'm fine.	– Gut.

❗ Im Gegensatz zu **How are you?** ist **How do you do?** eine Begrüßungsformel, auf die man mit **How do you do?** antwortet. Sie wird beim ersten Treffen in förmlichen Situationen verwendet.

2. Personal pronouns: it, we, they
Persönliche Fürwörter (→ Unit 1.2)

– What's your phone number?	– **It**'s 453 3468.

Im Englischen wird für Sachen **it** verwendet, für weibliche Personen **she** und für männliche Personen **he**.

– Where are **you** from?	**you**	Sie/ihr
– **We**'re from Liverpool.	**we**	wir
– Where are **Mrs Owen and her family** from?		
– **They**'re from Cardiff.	**they**	sie

Für **du, Sie, ihr** wird im Englischen immer **you** verwendet.

3. Possessive pronouns: his, her, our, their
Besitzanzeigende Fürwörter

This is Paul Owen.	**His** father's a dentist and **his** mother's a teacher.	**his**	sein seine
This is Jill Lennard.	**Her** son's a shop-assistant, **her** daughter's a clerk.	**her**	ihr ihre
Thomas, this is John,	**our** assistant manager.	**our**	unser
	What's **their** phone number?	**their**	ihre

Im Englischen werden **possessive pronouns** nicht verändert.

4. Personal and possessive pronouns: summary
Persönliche und besitzanzeigende Fürwörter: Zusammenfassung

		personal pronouns	possessive pronouns
1. Person	Einzahl	I	my
	Mehrzahl	we	our
2. Person	Einzahl	you	your
	Mehrzahl		
3. Person	Einzahl	he, she, it	his, her, (its)
	Mehrzahl	they	their

5. be: short forms and long forms
be: Kurzformen und Langformen

Brian's It's We're They're	Brian is It is We are They are	a shop-assistant. 453 3468. from Liverpool. from Cardiff.
short forms	long forms	

6. The indefinite article: a, an   Der unbestimmte Artikel

He's/She's a clerk. a secretary. a teacher.	Er/Sie ist Sachbearbeiter(in). Sekretär(in). Lehrer(in).
He's/She's an electrician. an assistant. an engineer.	Er/Sie ist Elektriker(in). Assistent(in). Ingenieur(in).

a: vor Wörtern, die mit **gesprochenem Mitlaut** (consonant), z. B. c, s, t, beginnen.

an: vor Wörtern, die mit **gesprochenem Selbstlaut** (vowel), a, e, i, o, u, beginnen.

❗ Im Gegensatz zum Deutschen steht vor Berufsbezeichnungen der unbestimmte Artikel **a, an.**

3 Unit

twenty 20

A 1 Schreiben Sie die Ländernamen und Nationalitätsbezeichnungen in die Leerzeilen zu den Städten:

	Land	Nationalität
 Zurich	a Switzerland	Swiss
 Paris	b France	French
 London	c Britain	British
 Innsbruck	d Austria	Austrian
 Heidelberg	e Germany	German

A 2 ↓ A 3

jemanden ansprechen: — Excuse me, …

Ortsangaben erfragen und machen:
– Are the German students here?
– Yes, they are./No, they aren't. They're at the hotel.

– … where's the business English course?
– It's in room 5.

– … where are the beginners?
– They're in room 1.

Wigton Language School · Room Plan

Room 1	Beginners
Room 2	Intermediate Course
Room 3	Advanced Group
Room 4	English for Secretaries
Room 5	Business English Course
Room 6	English for Engineers
Room 7	Conversation Group
Room 8	Refresher Course

A 2 → A 3

Eine Gruppe von Kursteilnehmern ist eben in der Wigton Language School eingetroffen. Alle fragen die Sekretärin, wo ihre verschiedenen Kurse stattfinden.
Ergänzen Sie Fragen und Antworten.

1. a – Excuse me, are the engineers in room 6?
   – Yes, _they are_.

   b – Excuse me, are the beginners in room 1?
   – Yes, _they're_.

   c – Excuse me, _are the_ secretaries in room 3?
   – No, _they're_. They _are_ in room 4.

2. a – Excuse me, where's the advanced group, please?
   – _It's in_ room 3.

   b – _Excuse me, where's_ the conversation group?
   – _It's in_ room 7.

   c – _Excuse me, where's_ the beginners, _please_?
   – _It's in_ room 1.

   d – _Excuse me, where's_ the business English course?
   – _It's in_ room 5.

3 Unit

twenty-two 22

A1 → A3

persönliche Informationen erfragen und geben (Nationalität, Herkunft, Beruf):

– Are you German?
– Yes, I am./No, I'm not. I'm Swiss.

– Is she from Austria?
– Yes, she is./No, she isn't. She's from Switzerland.

– Is he a student?
– No, he isn't. He's a teacher.

Auf der Fähre von Holyhead nach Dublin spricht eine irische Dame zwei Touristinnen an. Eine der beiden, Doris, führt das Gespräch (sie kann besser Englisch).

Mary: Hello, my name's Mary Bourke.
Doris: _Hello_, I'm Doris Schulze. And _this is_ Ulrike Brand.
Mary: Hello, Ulrike, nice _to meet you_.
Where _are_ you from?
Doris: _We're from_ Germany.
Are you English, Mary?
Mary: No, I'm _not_. I'm Irish!
Are you a student, Doris?
Doris: Yes, _I'm_. And you?
Mary: I'm _an_ engineer.
Doris: Oh, Ulrike _is an_ engineer, too.

A4 → A5

persönliche Informationen erfragen und geben (Wohnort):

– Where do you live?
– I live in Innsbruck.

– Where does Uwe live?
– He lives in Kiel.

– Where do Carla and Giovanni live?
– They live in Rome.

Doris: Where _do_ you live?

Mary: I _live_ in Liverpool. My father and mother _live in_ Dublin. And where _are you from_?

Doris: I'_m from_ Kiel.

Mary: _And_ Ulrike _is from_ Kiel, too?

Doris: No, _she's from_ Frankfurt.

A 6

nach Wünschen fragen:	– Would you like a single room or a double room?
Wünsche äußern:	– I'd/We'd like a double room with a bath, please.

Am Hotel-Empfang haben Sie ein Gespräch mitgehört. Numerieren Sie in der richtigen Reihenfolge.

Schreiben Sie das geordnete Gespräch ab, damit Sie in der Rechtschreibung sicherer werden.

Hotelangestellte:

___ – Good evening, sir.

___ – Yes, sir, room 10. Here's your key.

___ – Would you like a single room or a double room?

___ – Yes, sir, with a bath or a shower?

Gast:

___ – We'd like a double room, please.

___ – Thank you.

___ – Good evening. I'd like a room, please.

___ – With a shower, please.

Good evening, sir

Would you like a single room or a double room

Yes, sir, with a bath or a shower

Yes sir, room 10 Here's your key

Good evening. I'd like a room, please.

We'd like a double room, please

With a shower, please

Thank you

3 Unit

twenty-four 24

A 7 → A 8

persönliche Informationen erfragen und geben (Name, Adresse):	– What's your name, please? – Schneider. – What's your address? – I live in Duisburg, Bahnhofstraße 9.
Gesprächsablauf sichern (buchstabieren):	– How do you spell that, please?

Mary hat Doris und Ulrike eingeladen, sie bei ihrer Mutter in Dublin zu besuchen.

Doris: OK! What's _your_ address?

Mary: It's 24 Lassy Lane, Dublin.

Doris: Oh, how _do you_ spell that, please?

Mary: L – A – double S – Y   L – A – N – E.

Doris: Thanks. – Oh, what's _your_ name, please?

Mary: Milligan.

Doris: Err, _how do you_ spell _that_ ?

Mary: M – I – double L – I – G – A – N.

Doris: Thank you.

A 8 Welche Buchstaben im englischen Alphabet reimen sich?

a and: ____, ____

b and: _c_, _d_, _e_, ____, ____, ____, ____

q and: ____, ____

y and: ____

Hören Sie anschließend die Cassette zur Kontrolle.

Tonmaterialien zu ON THE WAY 1 – Arbeitsbuch

Die Compact-Cassette zum Arbeitsbuch enthält 19 vom Lehrbuch unabhängige Hörverständnistexte, mit deren Hilfe Sie auch zuhause das Verstehen von gesprochenem Englisch üben können. Die dazugehörigen Übungen sind im Arbeitsbuch mit dem Hörverständnissymbol gekennzeichnet.
Darüberhinaus finden Sie auf der Cassette Texte zur Lösungskontrolle einiger Ausspracheübungen.
Die Texte sind von britischen Muttersprachlern gesprochen.

Hiermit bestelle ich zur sofortigen Lieferung per Nachnahme

☐ **ON THE WAY 1 – Arbeitsbuch**
1 Compact-Cassette – Klett-Nr. 50016 – 18,80 DM ®

Laufgeschwindigkeit 4,75 cm/sek., Gesamtsprechzeit ca. 40 Minuten. Die Compact-Cassette ist auf beiden Seiten besprochen.

Lieferung durch jede Buchhandlung oder, wo dies auf Schwierigkeiten stößt, zuzüglich der Portokosten per Nachnahme vom Verlag. Preise freibleibend.
Stand vom 1.4.1986.

® unverb. Preisempf.

Ort und Datum

Unterschrift (des Erziehungsberechtigten)

Dieser Abschnitt gilt als Versandadresse; bitte deutlich schreiben →

Vorname, Name

Straße, Hausnummer

Postleitzahl, Wohnort

Compact-Cassette zu
ON THE WAY 1 – Arbeitsbuch

Sprecher: Peter Bartlett, John Graham, Eira Heath,
Anthony Hyde, Derrick Jenkins, Anne Rosenfeld, Coralyn Sheldon
Regie: Peter Bartlett und Ernst Klett Verlag
Tonstudio: Griffiths Hansen Recordings Ltd., London
Musik: Kuno Schmid

Compact-Cassette – Gesamtsprechzeit ca. 40 Minuten – Klett-Nr. 50016

Ernst Klett Stuttgart

Bitte als
Postkarte
frankieren

**Ernst Klett Verlag
Stuttgart**
Abt. Information und Beratung
Expeditionslager
Postfach 1170

7054 Korb

K 50015

25 twenty-five

Unit 3

A 9

Lösen Sie dieses Zahlenrätsel: Schreiben sie die angegebenen Zahlen in Buchstaben in die Kästchen. Die Schreibrichtung ist angezeigt.

65→ SIXTY-FIVE
55→ FIVE
13→ THIRTEEN
44→ FOURTY FOUR
22→ TWENTY-TWO
73→ SEVENTY-THREE
89→ EIGHTY-NINE
15→ FIFTEEN
90→ NINETY
12→ TWELVE
14→ FOURTEEN

Die Buchstaben in den blauen Kreisen ergeben – von unten nach oben gelesen – eine zweistellige Zahl:

twenty-one

B 1

Von der Cassette hören Sie ein kurzes Gespräch zwischen zwei Studenten der **Language School**, Anna Bessoni und Jacques Delon. Kreuzen Sie an, welche der folgenden Aussagen richtig (**true**) bzw. falsch (**false**) sind.

true / false

a Anna is Italian.
b She is a secretary.
c She is in the advanced group.
d Jacques is French.
e He is a secretary, too.
f He is on the refresher course.

3 Unit   twenty-six 26

B 2 Schreiben Sie die Geldbeträge in Zahlen und in Worten.

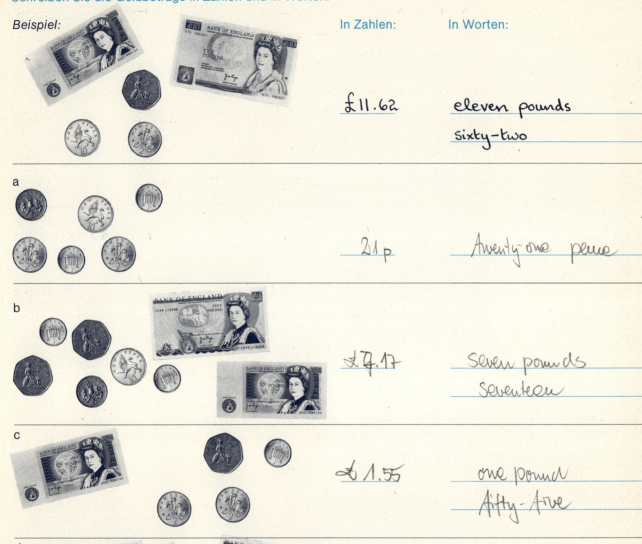

	In Zahlen:	In Worten:
Beispiel:	£11.62	eleven pounds sixty-two
a	21p	twenty-one pence
b	£7.17	seven pounds seventeen
c	£1.55	one pound fifty-five
d	£56.12	fifty-six pounds twelve

Unit 3

Beschreiben Sie diese Personen.

B 3

	Maria Gonzalez	Madrid	housewife
a	Karen Hinnekint	Rotterdam	secretary
b	Uwe Petersen Renate Petersen	Kiel	dentist dentist
c	Ian Thomas	Manchester	clerk
d	Artur Hügli	Berne	shop-assistant
e	Carla Vadini Giovanni Vadini	Rome	teacher engineer

Beispiel: Maria Gonzalez lives in Madrid. She's a housewife. In her free time she learns English.

a Karen Hinnekint lives in Rotterdam. She's a secretary. In her free time she works in the garden.

b Uwe and Renate Petersen live in in Kiel. They're dentists. In their free time they play tennis.

c Ian Thomas lives in Manchester. He's a clerk. In his free time he reads books.

d Artur Hügli lives in Berne. He's a shop-assistant. In his free time he plays foot-ball.

e Carla and Giovanni Vadini live in Rome. She's a teacher and he's an engineer. In their free time they watch television.

Unit 3 Grammar

1. Verbs and auxiliary verbs — Zeitwörter und Hilfszeitwörter

– **Is he** from Austria?
– Yes, **he is**.

Hilfszeitwörter wie **be** bilden die Frage wie im Deutschen durch Umstellung von Satzgegenstand *(subject)* und Hilfszeitwort.

No, I'm **not**.
No, we are**n't**.

Die Verneinung wird durch Hinzufügen von **not/n't** zum Hilfszeitwort gebildet.

Where **do** you **live**?

Zeitwörter (z. B. *live, spell*) benötigen zur Bildung der Frage immer ein Hilfszeitwort. Wenn kein anderes Hilfszeitwort im Satz vorhanden ist, wird die Frage mit dem Hilfszeitwort **do** gebildet.

2. Verbs: present simple — Zeitwörter: present simple

	Einzahl	Mehrzahl
1. Person	I live in Lausanne.	We (Carla and I) live in Rome.
3. Person	She (Claudia) live**s** in Innsbruck. He (Artur) live**s** in Berne.	They (Carla and Giovanni) live in Rome.

In der 3. Person Einzahl (z. B. he/Artur; she/Claudia) hat das Zeitwort die Endung **-s**.
Alle anderen Formen sind endungslos.

In his free time he watch**es** television.

Zeitwörter, die mit Zischlaut enden, haben in der 3. Person die Endung **-es**.

3. Auxiliary verb **do**: present simple — Hilfszeitwort **do**: present simple

– Where **do** you live?
– Where **does** Artur live?
– Where **do** Carla and Giovanni live?

– I live in Kiel.
– He lives in Berne.
– They live in Rome.

does { he/Artur
         she/Claudia

do bildet die 3. Person Einzahl mit der Endung **-es**.
Aussprache: **do** [duː/dʊ] aber **does** [dʌz/dəz].

4. Questions with question words + do

Im Englischen werden Fragesätze mit dem Hilfszeitwort **do** gebildet, wenn kein anderes Hilfszeitwort im Satz vorhanden ist.

Where do		Carla and Giovanni	live?	They		live	in Rome.
	Zeitwort	**Satzgegenstand ➡**	**Zeitwort**	**Satzgegenstand ➡**		**Zeitwort**	
Wo	wohnen	Carla und Giovanni?		Sie		wohnen	in Rom.

Im Gegensatz zum Deutschen bleibt im Englischen die Reihenfolge Satzgegenstand ➡ Zeitwort in Fragesätzen, die mit **do** gebildet werden, gleich der in Aussagesätzen.

– Where do**es** Claudia live? – She live**s** in Innsbruck.

In **do**-Fragen bleibt das Zeitwort unverändert.
In der 3. Person erhält **do** die Endung **-es**.

5. Yes/No questions with be and short answers
Entscheidungsfragen mit **be** und Kurzantworten

– **Are** you German?	– Yes, I am.	– No, I 'm not.
	– Yes, we are.	– No, we aren't.
– **Is** he from Austria?	– Yes, he is.	– No, he isn't.
– **Are** they students?	– Yes, they are.	– No, they aren't.

Fragen, auf die man mit **Yes** oder **No** antworten kann, beginnen immer mit einem Hilfszeitwort, z. B. einer Form von **be**.

 Die bejahenden Kurzantworten verwenden keine Kurzformen.

6. Short forms

No, **I'm** not.
I'd/We'd like a room.
He/She **isn't** Swiss.
They **aren't** German.
Oh, **you're** Swiss!

No, I am not.
I/We would like a room.
He/She is not Swiss.
They are not German.
Oh, you are Swiss!

7. The definite article: the — Der bestimmte Artikel

the	refresher course	der Auffrischungskurs	Im Gegensatz zum Deutschen gibt es im Englischen nur eine Form des bestimmten Artikels: **the**.
the	advanced group	die Fortgeschrittenengruppe	
the	class register	das Klassenverzeichnis	
the	engineer	der Ingenieur	
the	engineers	die Ingenieure	

Aussprache

the [ðə] **b**eginners the [ðə] **c**onversation group	[ðə] vor **gesprochenen Mitlauten** wie b, c, r, ...
the [ðɪ] **a**dvanced group the [ðɪ] **i**ntermediate course	[ðɪ] vor den **gesprochenen Selbstlauten a, e, i, o, u**

8. Plural forms of nouns — Mehrzahlformen von Hauptwörtern

Die Mehrzahlform der Hauptwörter wird normalerweise durch Anfügen von **-s** an die Einzahlform gebildet.

book student	book**s** student**s**	[s] Nach gesprochenem [p, t, k, θ, f] wird das Mehrzahl **-s** stimmlos (zischend) ausgesprochen.
beginner friend	beginner**s** friend**s**	[z] Nach fast allen anderen Mitlauten wird es stimmhaft (summend) ausgesprochen.
❗ secreta**ry**	secretar**ies**	Hauptwörter, die auf **Mitlaut + y** enden, bilden die Mehrzahl mit **ies**.

Unit 4

jemanden nach dem Weg fragen:	– Where's the nearest …? Is there a … near here?

Orts-/Richtungsangaben machen:	– Go straight on and turn right into King Street.
	  Turn right at the corner.
	  It's over there on the left.
	  It's opposite Sidoli's Café.
	  There's one in Town Street.

A 1 ↓ A 2

1. Was bedeuten diese Verkehrsschilder auf englisch?

a _turn left_.

b _turn right_.

c _go straight on_.

2. Fill in: at, in (3x), into, near (2x)

a The Business English course is _in_ room 5.
b I live _in_ Brokdorf, a town _near_ Hamburg.
c Turn left _at_ the corner.
d Is there a bus stop _near_ here?
e There's a bookshop _in_ Victoria Lane.
f Turn right _into_ Victoria Lane.

3. a – Where's the nearest phone-box?

– There's one _in_ New Street,
  next to the post office,
  opposite the railway station.

b – Where's the nearest bus stop?

– There's one _in_ High Street,
  near the tourist information office.

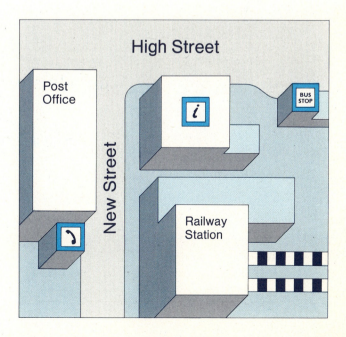

4 Unit

thirty-two 32

A 3  first 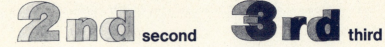 second  third

Where's the exit?

a Turn _left_ here, then turn _right_ at the _second_ corner and _left_ at the _third corner_; the exit is then _straight on_.

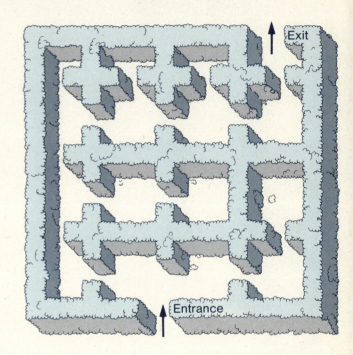

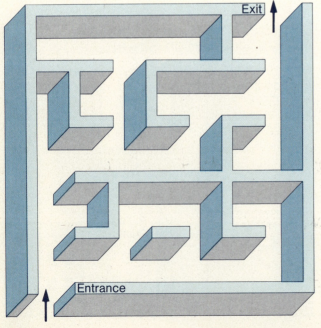

b Go _straight_ and turn _right_ into the _third_ lane. Then _turn left at the second corner, then right, then left and the exit is straight on_.

Unit 4

A 2 ↓ A 4

jemanden nach dem Weg fragen:	– Is there a/an ... near here?
Orts-/Richtungsangaben machen:	– Yes, there's one ...
Ungewißheit ausdrücken:	– I think ...
Bedauern/Unwissen ausdrücken:	– Sorry, I don't know.

Schauen Sie die Karte zu A 1 im Lehrbuch (Seite 30) noch einmal an.
Ein Ortsfremder fragt Sie, wo bestimmte Gebäude sind. Beantworten Sie seine Fragen anhand der Karte. (Sie sind in der **Station Road**. Die Stelle ist auf der Karte markiert.)

Beispiel:
– Excuse me, is there a phone-box near here?
– Yes, I think there's one in Park Road. Go straight on here, turn right at Barclays Bank, and the phone box is on your right.
– Thank you.

Die weiteren Gebäude, nach denen er fragt, sind: a café, b police station, c toilet, d hotel, e pub

a – Excuse me, _is there a_ café near here?
– I think _there's one in_ King Street. Go _straight on here, turn right_ at the bus stop, and the café's _on your right_.
– _____.

b – _Excuse me, is there a police station near here. Sorry, I don't know_?
– _____.

c – _Excuse me, is there a toilet near here. Yes there's one in_?
– Yes, _Market Lane over there on the left_.
– _____.

d – _Excuse me is there a hotel near here. Yes there's one in_?
– _Market Lane. Turn left here and the Station hotel is on your left, opposite the Odeon Cinema._
– _____.

e – _Excuse me is there a pub near here. Yes there's one_?
– _Sorry, I don't know._

4 Unit

A 5

| nach etwas fragen (Gebäude/Straßen etc.): | – Is this London Bridge? ... And what's that over there? |
| etwas benennen: | – That's Tower Bridge. |

Ergänzen Sie die Gespräche in den Bildgeschichten.

a **Metropole Hotel**

b **At the pub**

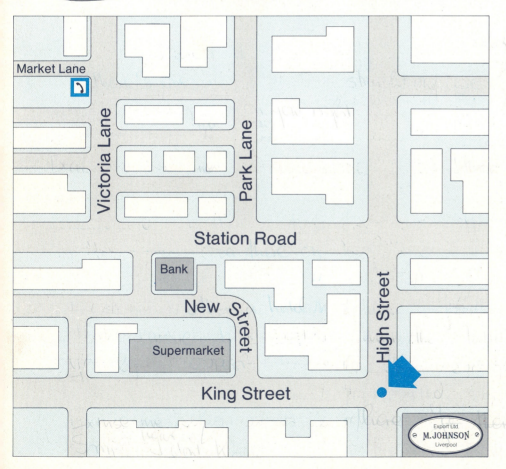

Simon Harris lädt Thomas Müller zu einer Party bei sich ein. Er erklärt ihm, wie man vom Büro aus (King Street/Ecke High Street) hinkommt. Hören Sie das Gespräch und markieren Sie den Weg auf der Karte.

B 1

4 Unit

thirty-six 36

B 1
↓
B 3

Ein Besucher der Firma Johnson Export Ltd trifft Ann Francis auf dem Treppeneingang. Er fragt sie, in welchem Zimmer er einen Mitarbeiter findet. Ergänzen Sie die Gespräche nach dem Beispiel.

Beispiel:

Besucher: Excuse me, where's Mr Harris, please?
Ann Francis: Mr Harris? He's in room five. Turn right and his office is the second on the right.
Besucher: Thanks.

a – Excuse me, **where's** Thomas Müller, please?
 – The new assistant from Germany? **He's** in room **4**.
  Turn **right** and **his** office is the **third** on the left.
 – Thank you.

b – **Excuse** me, **where's** June Taylor, **please**?
 – June? **She's in** room **6**. Turn **right** and **her** office is here at the corner, the first **(room) on the right**.
 – **Thank you**.

Unit 4

c – Where's the general manager, _please_?
– Mr Morrison? _He's_ room _1_ – the _second_ office on _the left_.
– _Excuse me_.

d – _Where's_, _____ John Wilson, please?
– John Wilson? _He's in_ room _2_. _His_ office is straight _on_, over _there_.
– _Thanks_.

e – _Excuse me, where's_ Ann Francis, _please_?
– Here – I'm Ann Francis!

The Thomas family: Mr and Mrs Thomas, three daughters and two sons. Nancy is a shop-assistant and Alan is an electrician. Susan is thirteen, Joan is nine and Ian is a baby.

B 4

		true	false
a	The first son in the Thomas family is an electrician.	X	
b	Susan is the first daughter in the family.		X
c	Joan is the third daughter in the family.	X	
d	The second daughter in the family is nine.		X
e	Ian is the second son in the family.	X	

4 Unit Grammar

thirty-eight 38

1. Demonstrative pronouns: this, that   Hinweisende Fürwörter

| – Is **this** London Bridge?
– Yes, it is.
– And what's **that** over there?
– **That**'s Tower Bridge. | – Ist dies hier die London Bridge?
– Ja.
– Und was ist das da drüben?
– Das ist die Tower Bridge. |

This verweist auf Personen/Sachen, die dem Sprecher vergleichsweise näher sind.
That verweist auf Personen/Sachen, die vom Sprecher vergleichsweise weiter entfernt sind.

❗ Nach gesprochenem **-s** am Wortende wird keine Kurzform gebildet, da diese schwierig auszusprechen wäre. Daher **this is**, aber **that's**.

2. Yes/No questions with Is this ...? and short answers   Entscheidungsfragen mit Is this ...? und Kurzantworten

| – **Is this** London Bridge? | – Yes, **it** is.
– No, **it** isn't. |

This/That in Fragen werden in der Kurzantwort durch **it** aufgegriffen.

3. Yes/No questions with Is there ...?

| – **Is there** a phone-box near here?
– Yes, **there's** one in New Street. | – Gibt es hier in der Nähe eine Telefonzelle?
– Ja, es gibt eine in der New Street. |

Der englische Ausdruck **there's** entspricht meist dem deutschen **es gibt**.

4. Prop word: one   Stützwort

| – Excuse me. Where's the nearest **post office**?
– There's **one** in King Street. |

Das Stützwort **one** wird verwendet, um die Wiederholung eines Hauptworts zu vermeiden.

5. Proper names with and without the   Eigennamen mit und ohne the

| **The** Station Hotel is opposite the cinema.
the National Gallery
the Houses of Parliament |

the steht vor Eigennamen von Hotels, Theatern, Kinos und Museen sowie vor Eigennamen in der Mehrzahl.

| Turn right at Barclays Bank.
Go down Station Road.
You are on Westminster Bridge. |

the steht **nicht** vor Eigennamen von Straßen, Plätzen, Parks, Gebäuden.

❗ the Strand

6. Imperative   Aufforderungs- und Befehlsform

| **Go** straight on and turn right into King Street. | Gehen/Fahren Sie geradeaus und biegen Sie rechts in die King Street ab. |

Im Englischen wird der **imperative** ohne persönliches Fürwort gebildet.

Unit 5

jemanden nach der Uhrzeit fragen:	– What's the time, please?/ Can you tell me the time, please?
Zeitangaben machen:	– It's seven o'clock/half past nine/ almost quarter to three/five past ten/twenty-five to eleven.

A 1
↓
A 2

1. What's the time here?

a Edinburgh

It's _ten_ past _eight_ in _Edinburgh_

b Nuremberg

It's _ten_ past _nine_ in _Nuremberg_

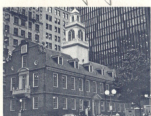

c Boston

It's _ten_ past _three_ in _Boston_

d Bombay

In _Bombay_ it's _twenty to two_

2. Hören Sie Gespräche mit, in denen es um die Uhrzeit geht. Kreuzen Sie an, wieviel Uhr es ist.

a It's ☐ quarter past five.
      ☐ quarter to nine.
      ☐ quarter past nine.

b It's almost ☐ ten to seven.
              ☐ ten to ten.
              ☐ ten past seven.

c It's ☐ ten past eight
      ☐ eight o'clock   in New York.
      ☐ one o'clock

It's ☐ 00.00
     ☐ 12.00   in London now.
     ☐ 13.00

And it's ☐ 🕐
         ☐ 🕐   in Augsburg.
         ☐ 🕐

3. Ergänzen Sie die Fragen nach der Uhrzeit.

a Excuse _me_, can _you tell me the time_, please?

b _Excuse me_, what's _the time_, _please_?

5 Unit

forty 40

A 3 → A 4

persönliche Informationen erfragen und geben (Geburtstag): — When's your birthday?

Zeitangaben machen (Monatstage, Uhrzeiten): — The 8th of December is Paul's birthday.
On the 15th there is a concert at 7 o'clock.

1. **Ergänzen Sie Zahlen und Daten mit Hilfe der Liste von US-Präsidenten auf Seite 41.**

Beispiel:

The _thirteenth_ of April is Thomas Jefferson's birthday.

Jefferson: the _third_ US president.

a The _thirty-second_ US president: Franklin D. Roosevelt.
 – When's his birthday?
 – The _thirtieth_ of January.

b – When's President Wilson's birthday?
 – _The twenty-eighth of_ December.
 Woodrow Wilson: _the twenty-eighth_ US president.

c John Quincy Adams: _sixth_ US president.
 – When's his birthday?
 – _the eleventh of July_.

2. **Auf dem Kalenderblatt sind einige Tage markiert, die für die USA besonders wichtig sind: Abraham Lincolns Geburtstag, der Valentinstag und George Washingtons Geburtstag. Ergänzen Sie die folgenden Angaben mit Hilfe des Kalenderblattes und der Liste der US-Präsidenten.**

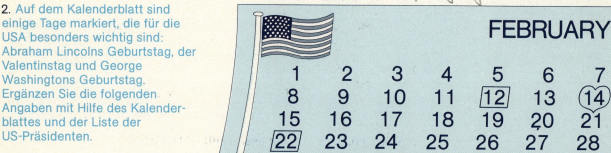

THE PRESIDENTS OF THE USA

Name	Born
1. George Washington	1732, Feb. 22
2. John Adams	1735, Oct. 30
3. Thomas Jefferson	1743, Apr. 13
4. James Madison	1751, Mar. 16
5. James Monroe	1758, Apr. 28
6. John Quincy Adams	1767, July 11
7. Andrew Jackson	1767, Mar. 15
8. Martin Van Buren	1782, Dec. 5
9. William Henry Harrison	1773, Feb. 9
10. John Tyler	1790, Mar. 29
11. James Knox Polk	1795, Nov. 2
12. Zachary Taylor	1784, Nov. 24
13. Millard Fillmore	1800, Jan. 7
14. Franklin Pierce	1804, Nov. 23
15. James Buchanan	1791, Apr. 23
16. Abraham Lincoln	1809, Feb. 12
17. Andrew Johnson	1808, Dec. 29
18. Ulysses Simpson Grant	1822, Apr. 27
19. Rutherford Birchard Hayes	1822, Oct. 4
20. James Abram Garfield	1831, Nov. 19
21. Chester Alan Arthur	1830, Oct. 5
22. Grover Cleveland	1837, Mar. 18
23. Benjamin Harrison	1833, Aug. 20
24. Grover Cleveland	1837, Mar. 18
25. William McKinley	1843, Jan. 29
26. Theodore Roosevelt	1858, Oct. 27
27. William Howard Taft	1857, Sept. 15
28. Woodrow Wilson	1857, Dec. 28
29. Warren Gamaliel Harding	1865, Nov. 2
30. Calvin Coolidge	1872, July 4
31. Herbert Clark Hoover	1874, Aug. 10
32. Franklin Delano Roosevelt	1882, Jan. 30
33. Harry S. Truman	1884, May 8
34. Dwight David Eisenhower	1890, Oct. 14
35. John F. Kennedy	1917, May 29
36. Lyndon Baines Johnson	1908, Aug. 27
37. Richard Milhous Nixon	1913, Jan. 9
38. Gerald R. Ford	1913, July 14
39. James Earl Carter	1924, Oct. 1
40. Ronald Reagan	1911, Feb. 6

a The _twelfth_ of February is Lincoln's _birthday_.
Abraham Lincoln: the _sixteenth_ US president.

b The _fourteenth of February_ is St Valentine's Day.

c _The twenty-second of February_ is George Washington's _birthday_.
Washington: _the first_ president.

3. Im Lehrbuch, Abschnitt A 3 (Seite 40), finden Sie Informationen über wichtige Feiertage. Beantworten Sie dazu diese Fragen:

a – Is Christmas Eve on the twenty-fifth of December?
 – _No, it isn't_. It's _on the twenty-fourth of December_.

b – When's New Year's Eve?
 – _It's on the thirty-first of December_.

c – Is Christmas Day the twenty-fifth of December?
 – _yes, it is_.

Unit 5

forty-two 42

A 5 → A 6

jemanden nach etwas fragen:	– Have you got a map of Edinburgh?
eine Frage bejahen:	– Yes, we have.
eine Frage verneinen:	– No, (I'm sorry), we haven't.
Sachinformationen erfragen und geben (Preise):	– How much is it? – It's £1.50./It's free.

1. Philip und Brenda Brown machen einmal im Jahr eine große Einkaufsfahrt nach London, um ihre Weihnachtsgeschenke zu kaufen. Bevor sie losfahren, fragen sie einander, ob sie alles mithaben. Was sie schon bereitgelegt haben, sehen Sie im Bild links.

Brenda: Have you got your keys?

Philip: Oh, no, __I haven't__.

Have __you__ got your Christmas shopping list?

Brenda: __Yes__, __I have__.

And __have you got__ our map of London?

Philip: __Yes__, __I have__.

__And have you got__ the address of the tea shop?

Brenda: __Yes__, __I have__.

__And have you got__ Jenny's phone number?

Philip: __Yes__, __I have__.

Unit 5

2. Kundengespräch im Spirituosengeschäft: Welches sind die korrekten und angemessenen Antworten des Verkäufers?

i. Have you got 'Johnny Walker Black Label' whisky?

- a ☐ Yes, here.
- b ☒ Yes, we have, madam. Here you are.
- c ☐ Yes, please.

ii. Have you got 'Gordon's Dry Gin', too?

- a ☐ No, we haven't.
- b ☐ No.
- c ☒ No, I'm sorry, we haven't.

iii. OK, how much is the whisky?

- a ☐ Fine, thanks.
- b ☐ Not so bad.
- c ☒ It's £9.50.

A 7

Sachinformationen erfragen und geben (Preise, Fahrzeiten, Abfahrtzeiten):	– How much is the tour to Torquay? – That's £5.05. – What time does the coach leave? – It leaves at 8 o'clock in the morning. – How long does it take? – About 12 hours.

Auf der nächsten Seite finden Sie drei **Coach Tours**-Angebote. Sehen Sie sie genau an und machen Sie dann die Übung auf Seite 45.

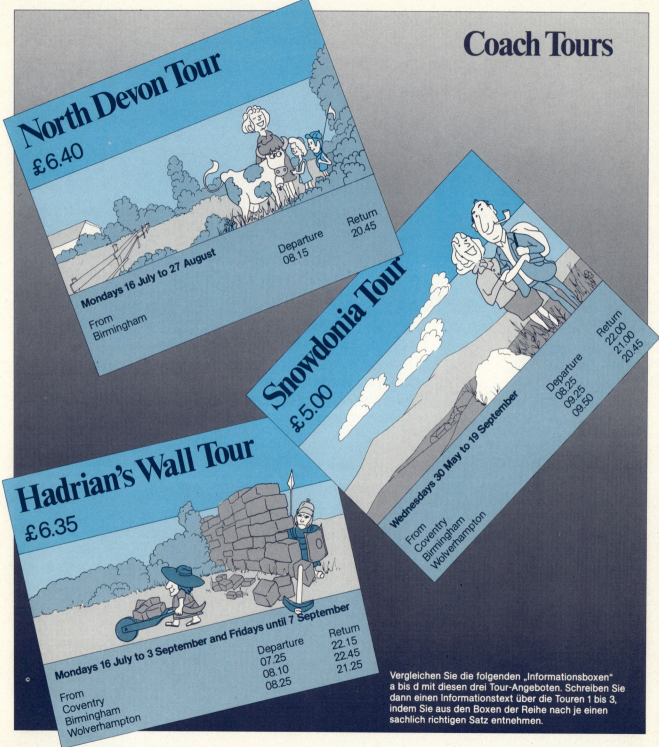

Unit 5

| a | 1. The North Devon Tour
2. The Snowdonia Tour
3. The Hadrian's Wall Tour | takes | 11 hours
about 14 hours
12 hours | from Birmingham. |

| b | The coach leaves Birmingham | at 8.15
at 9.25
at 8.10 | on | Wednesdays.
Mondays.
Mondays and Fridays. |

| c | It returns to Birmingham | at 9 o'clock
at 10.45
at 8.45 | in the evening. |

| d | The North Devon Tour
The Snowdonia Tour
The Hadrian's Wall Tour | is | £6.35
£5.00
£6.40 | per person. |

Schreiben Sie hier:

1. a The North Devon Tour takes about 12 hours from Birmingham.
   b The coach _leaves Birmingham at 8.15 on Mondays_.
   c It _returns to Birmingham at 8.45 in the evening_.
   d The _North Devon Tour is £6.40 per person_.

2. a The Snowdonia Tour _takes about 11 hours from Birmingham_.
   b _The coach leaves Birmingham at 9.25 on Wednesdays_.
   c _It returns to Birmingham at 9 o'clock in the evening_.
   d _The Snowdonia Tour is £5.00 per person_.

3. a The Hadrian's Wall Tour _takes about 14 hours from Birmingham_.
   b _The coach leaves Birmingham at 8.10 on Mondays and Fridays_.
   c _It returns to Birmingham at 10.45 in the evening_.
   d _the Tour is £6.35 per person_.

5 Unit

forty-six 46

B 1 ↓ B 2 Beurteilen Sie, welche der folgenden „Informationen" über das **Cambridge Festival** bzw. das **Cambridge Folk Festival** (nicht) stimmen. Benutzen Sie dabei die Programmauszüge in B 1 und B 2 (Lehrbuch, S. 43/44) als Grundlage.
Bitte kreuzen Sie an und korrigieren Sie falsche Informationen auf den Leerzeilen.

true / false

a 'Richard III' is on at 7.45 p.m. on Wednesday, July 15th. — X

b 'Ballet for All' is on at the Arts Theatre at 8.15 p.m. on July 15th. X —

c 'The Caretaker' is at 5.30 p.m. and 9.30 p.m. on July 15th. — X

d Tickets for the Arts Theatre are £3.50, £2.00 and 95p. — X

e Tickets for 'Much Ado About Nothing' are £1.75 and £1.00. — X

true / false

a The fourth Cambridge Folk Festival is on the weekend of July 28th, 29th, 30th. — X

b There is a promenade concert on the twenty-seventh of July. X —

c Tom Paxton is on at 6.15 a.m. on the twenty-ninth of July. — X

d On the thirty-first of July, the Red Clay Ramblers are on.

e Billy Connolly is on at 11.30 a.m. on the twenty-ninth of July.

f What time are Pete & Chris Coe on? – At half past ten.

g How much is a weekend ticket? – Sixteen pounds fifty.

Unit 5

Von den folgenden Satzpaaren hören Sie von der Cassette nur je einen Satz zweimal. Entscheiden Sie, welcher Satz jeweils gesprochen wurde und unterstreichen Sie ihn.

B 1
↓
B 3

1. a Where's Susan?

   Here's Susan!

   b Is he English?

   Is she English?

   c They're three.

   They're free.

   d Hello, Alan.

   Hello, Ellen.

2. a Mrs Lennard's over there.

   Mr Lennard's over there.

   b It's the 3rd street on the left.

   It's the 1st street on the left.

   c I'm in Room 13.

   I'm in Room 30.

   d How do you spell your first name?

   E – l – s – a.

   I – l – s – e.

3. a On the thirtieth of July, Diz Disley's on.

   On the thirteenth of July, Diz Disley's on.

   b Tickets are available on Monday and Tuesday.

   Tickets are available on Monday and Thursday.

   c The Ford Cortina costs £17 for 5 days.

   The Ford Cortina costs £70 for 5 days.

   d No, I'm sorry, we haven't. But we've got a Mini.

   No, I'm sorry, I haven't. But I've got a Mini.

5 Unit Grammar

1. Questions with can

Can you tell me the time, please?
Can I help you?

Können Sie mir bitte sagen, wie spät es ist?
Kann ich Ihnen helfen?

Die Frage mit **can** wird hier zum höflichen Ausdruck einer Bitte/Aufforderung bzw. eines Angebots verwendet.

2. Questions with question words: how much?, how long?

- **How much** is it?
- **How much** does it cost?
- **How long** does it take?

- It's free.
- It's £7.40.
- About 12 hours.

- Wieviel kostet es?
- Wieviel kostet es?
- Wie lange dauert es?

- Nichts.
- £7.40.
- Ungefähr 12 Stunden.

3. Yes/No questions with have got and short answers

Have you **got** a map of Scotland?

Yes, we **have**.
No, we **haven't**.

Haben Sie eine Karte von Schottland?

Ja.
Nein.

In der Bedeutung **haben/besitzen** steht im gesprochenen Englisch und in persönlichen Briefen die Form **have got**. In der Kurzantwort entfällt **got**.

4. Short forms

haven't ← have not

5. The position of the adverbials of place and time
Die Stellung der Umstandsbestimmungen des Ortes und der Zeit

There is a concert **at 8 p.m.**
It's 1 o'clock **in London**.

Umstandsbestimmungen des Ortes und der Zeit stehen meist am Satzende.

On the 15th there is a concert at 7 o'clock.
On the 23rd there is a tea party at 4 o'clock.

In Frankfurt it's one o'clock.
In New York it's seven o'clock.

Umstandsbestimmungen des Ortes und der Zeit können aber auch am Satzanfang stehen, wenn z. B. Orte einander gegenübergestellt oder Termine aufgezählt werden sollen.

Grammar Unit 5

6. Personal pronouns: subject case – object case
Persönliche Fürwörter als Satzgegenstand – als Ergänzung

						subject case	object case
Can	you	tell	me	the time, please?			
Can	I	help	you?			I	me
	subject case	verb Zeitwort	object case			you	you

Persönliche Fürwörter stehen im Englischen als Satzgegenstand vor, als Ergänzung nach dem Zeitwort.

7. 's–genitive and of–genitive

The 8th of December is Paul's birthday.

The 20th of December is the 1st day of the Christmas holidays.

Der Genitiv mit 's gibt an, welcher **Person** etwas gehört oder zugeordnet ist.

Der Genitiv mit **of** gibt an, welcher **Sache** etwas zugeordnet ist.

"Is that the time?"

6 Unit

A 1 ↓ A 3

jemanden nach seinen Plänen fragen:	– What are you doing after the lesson?
eine Einladung aussprechen:	– Would you like to go for a drink?
eine Einladung annehmen:	– Yes, I'd love to./That's a good idea!
eine Einladung ablehnen und dies begründen:	– No, I'm sorry, I can't. I'm working late this evening.
etwas vorschlagen (Termin):	– Is 7.30 all right?/What about Tuesday?
einen Vorschlag annehmen:	– Yes, fine.

Ein englischer Bekannter lädt Sie zum Essen ein. Wählen Sie die jeweils bestgeeignete Antwort.

1. *Engländer:* Would you like to come to dinner next week?

   Sie: a ☒ Yes, I'd love to. When?
   b ☐ Yes, I'd love to. What time?
   c ☐ Yes, that's fine.

2. *Engländer:* What about Friday?

   Sie: a ☐ No, I can't come on Friday.
   b ☐ Friday …? No, I'm sorry.
   c ☒ I'm sorry, I can't. I'm going to London on Friday.

3. *Engländer:* What about Thursday, then?

   Sie: a ☐ Sorry, I can't.
   b ☒ Fine, what time?
   c ☐ Yes, I'd love to.

4. *Engländer:* Is 6.30 all right?
   Sie: Yes, that's fine.
   Engländer: Good. And you can meet my wife Alice then.

   Sie: a ☐ Nice to meet you.
   b ☒ Fine, see you on Thursday, then.
   c ☐ Yes, thanks.

Zu einem späteren Zeitpunkt lädt er Sie dann ins Kino ein:

5. *Engländer:* What are you doing this evening?

   Sie: a ☐ Yes, I am.
   b ☒ Nothing special.
   c ☐ No, I'm sorry, I can't.

6. *Engländer:* Would you like to go to the cinema?

   Sie: a ☒ That's a good idea!
   b ☐ Thank you.
   c ☐ That's all right.

Unit 6

A 4

nach Gründen fragen: – Why can't Frank and Mary go out?

etwas begründen: – Because the weather's so wet.

Ergänzen Sie das Gespräch mit Hilfe der Abbildungen.

Anne: Bill, we can't have our party this Saturday.

Bill: Why can't we have it on Saturday?

Anne: Because our friends can't come then.

Bill: Why can't John come?

Anne: Because he's playing football.

Bill: And why can't Liz come?

Anne: Because she's working on Saturday evening.

Bill: And why can't Thomas come?

Anne: Because he's going to Canterb. for the weekend.

Bill: And why can't Graham and Susan come?

Anne: Because they're going to the theatre.

Bill: Hmm. Well, what about dinner for two at the new French restaurant in town?
Anne: Oh, fine!

Wortschatzübung
Hier werden die Freizeitbeschäftigungen einiger Personen angegeben. Aber ein Wort in jeder Reihe ist Unsinn. Streichen Sie es aus und benutzen Sie es, um einen zweiten Satz zu bilden.

Beispiel: In his free time Jim plays tennis, ~~television~~ and football.
Ann watches television.

a In her free time Doris learns Italian, Dutch and ~~books~~.
Mary reads book.

b In their free time the Browns watch TV, films and magazines.
The Morrisons read magazines.

c In his free time George goes for a walk, a swim, a garden or a drink.
Tom walks in the garden.

d In her free time Susan reads books, the newspaper, magazines and the theatre.
Robert goes to the theatre.

A 1
↓
A 5

6 Unit

A 5
↓
A 6

um Erlaubnis bitten:	– Can I borrow your magazine, please?
fragen, ob etwas erlaubt ist:	– Can I park here?
Erlaubnis gewähren:	– Yes, of course./Yes, sure.
Bedauern ausdrücken: ein Verbot ausdrücken:	– No, I'm afraid you can't. It's not allowed.
sich bedanken:	– Thank you./Thanks.
auf Dank reagieren:	– That's OK.

Von der Cassette hören Sie fünf kurze Gespräche. Entscheiden Sie, ob ein Gespräch bei Bekannten oder unter Fremden stattfindet und kreuzen Sie dann das entsprechende Kästchen an. Hören Sie zuerst ein Beispiel: – Hello.
– Hello, John. What about a drink?

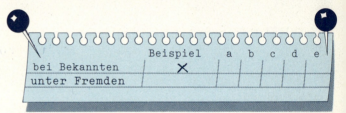

B 1 Crossword Puzzle (Kreuzworträtsel)

ACROSS →
4. the weekend = ... and Sunday
12. man's name
14. "Please close the ... "

DOWN ↓
1. street = r ... d
2. job: TV ... master
3. " ... like to rent a car."
4. "We can't go for a swim because the ...'s so cold."
5. you're = you ...
7. "... morning."
8. "What's your ...?" – "Elsa."
9. "... you later!"
11. In school we learn to ... and write.
12. Sue and Dave live ... Bristol.
13. "Can I smoke here?" – "Sure, why ...?"
14. you and I
15. "This food is ... bad, I can't eat it."

53 fifty-three

Unit 6

B 2

1. Die Studentin Inge hat eine Brieffreundschaft mit der jungen englischen Übersetzerin June angefangen. June schickt diesen Brief mit 4 Photos an Inge, aber sie hat vergessen, die Photos entsprechend der Beschreibung im Brief zu numerieren. Können Sie die Photos numerieren?

January 15th

Dear Inge,

Here are some photos of my family, my friend and me.

Photo no. 1: My friend and I are going for a swim. Our town is near the sea.

In the second photo you see my father and mother and me on the beach in August. It's dirty here at the end of the summer. Why do people leave their newspapers, food etc. on the beach?

No. 3: This is my room. In my free time I read books or watch TV here. What do you do in your free time?

No 4: This is my office at the export firm. It's not very far from our house.

What are you doing this summer? Would you like to visit us? I'd love to meet you.

Yours sincerely,

June

B 2 2. Inge schreibt den folgenden Brief zurück. Ergänzen Sie ihn mit den Ausdrücken aus der Worttafel.

February 3

Dear June,

Thanks for the photos and the invitation to visit you. _I'd love to_ come, but I'm sorry, _I can't_ because _I'm working_ this summer. _I've got_ a summer job from July till September: an English firm here needs a German typist.

What do _I do_ in my free time? _I play_ tennis. And _I watch_ the English and American films on our "third programme" on TV. Are there German films on British television?

Hoping to hear from you again soon,

Yours sincerely,

Inge

I'm working	I've got	I can't
I'd love to	I play	I do	I watch

Unit 6

An invitation B 3

Lesen Sie den Brief an Joan und hören Sie anschließend das Telefongespräch zwischen Joan und Joe auf der Cassette. Dann kreuzen Sie **true** (richtig) oder **false** (falsch) an und korrigieren Sie falsche Informationen auf den Leerzeilen.

> 14/9/81
>
> Dear Joan,
>
> Friday's my birthday and we're having a party at our flat in the evening. Would you like to come? All my friends from the office and some of Kate's colleagues are coming.
>
> Please let us know if you can come too.
>
> Love,
> Joe and Kate

true / false

a Joe and Kate live in Manchester. _____
b Friday is Kate's birthday. _____
c Joe's colleagues are coming to the party.
   _____
d Joan can come to the party, too. _____
e Her friends are coming on the 8th.
   _____
f The friends are German.
   _____
g Joan speaks German. _____
h Joan and Joe go to an evening class. _____

Word game (Wortspiel) B 4
Wie viele englische Wörter können Sie aus den Buchstaben des Wortes INVITATIONS bilden?

I, in, to, on, inn, so, Ain, no, uation, son, an visit, station

Wir fanden 12 Wörter mit 1, 2 oder 3 Buchstaben, ein Wort mit 4 Buchstaben und ein Wort mit 7 Buchstaben, die Sie alle im Lauf des Kurses schon gelernt haben.

Unit Grammar

1. Questions with would

– **Would** you like to come to dinner on Sunday?
– Yes, I'd love to./No, I'm sorry, I can't.

– Möchten Sie am Sonntag zum Essen kommen?
– Ja, gerne./Nein, ich kann leider nicht.

Die Frage mit **would** wird hier zum höflichen Ausdruck einer Einladung verwendet.

2. Questions with question words and answers: why? – because

– **Why** can't Sarah play on the beach?
– **Because** it's so dirty.

– **Why** do people learn English?
– **Because** they want to go to Britain.

3. Main clauses and subclauses + conjunction: because
Haupt- und Nebensätze + Bindewort

| We can't go out | **because** the weather's so wet. |
| They can't sleep | **because** there's so much noise. |

| main clause | conjunction + subclause |
| Hauptsatz | Bindewort + Nebensatz |

4. Short forms: can't

can't ⬅ can~~not~~

❗ Aussprache: **can** [kæn/kən], aber **can't** [kɑːnt]

5. Verbs: present continuous (form)   Die Bildung des present continuous

I	'm/am	go**ing**.
We	're/are	leav**ing**.
	Form von **be**	Zeitwort + **ing**

Ein **nicht gesprochenes -e** am Ende eines Zeitworts **entfällt** bei Anfügung von **-ing**: leav**e** ➡ lea**v**ing.

6. Present continuous with future meaning
Present continuous zum Ausdruck zukünftigen Geschehens

– What are you doing after the lesson? – We're meeting friends. – When are you going to London? – We're leaving on the 21st.	– Was machst du/machen Sie macht ihr nach dem Unterricht? – Wir treffen uns mit Freunden. – Wann fährst du/fahren Sie fahrt ihr nach London? – Wir fahren am 21.

Das **present continuous** drückt hier aus, daß eine Handlung im Augenblick des Sprechens für die Zukunft fest geplant ist.

Der Zeitpunkt der Handlung geht entweder aus dem Gesprächszusammenhang hervor oder wird durch eine Zeitbestimmung – **after the lesson, tomorrow, on Tuesday, on the 21st** – festgelegt.

7. Verbs + to-infinitive: like to – love to – want to
Zeitwörter und die Grundform mit **to**

– Would you	**like**	**to come**?	
– Yes, I'd	**love**	**to (come)**.	
– They	**want**	**to go**	to Britain.
	Zeitwort + **to** + Zeitwort		

Nach Zeitwörtern, die einen Wunsch oder Plan ausdrücken, folgt sehr häufig eine Grundform mit vorangestelltem **to**.

8. Personal pronouns: subject case – object case (➔ Unit 5.6)

We're having a party.	subject case	**we**
Please let **us** know if you can come.	object case	**us**

7 Unit

fifty-eight 58

A 1

jemanden nach dem Weg fragen:	– Where can I find postcards, please?
Orts-/Richtungsangaben machen:	– Postcards are on the ground floor.
Sachinformationen erfragen:	– Do you sell stamps, too?
eine Frage bejahen:	– Yes, sir/madam. ...
eine Frage verneinen:	– No, we don't.

Dominoes

Bilden Sie kurze Gespräche zwischen Kaufhaus-
angestellten und Kunden, indem Sie jeweils
3–4 Dominosteine in einer sinnvollen Reihenfolge
zusammensetzen und schreiben Sie diese Gespräche
auf ein Blatt Papier. Dabei können Sie manche Steine
in mehreren Gesprächen verwenden.
Wir fanden 5 sinnvolle Gespräche.

Beispiel: 1 – 7 – 5
– Excuse me, where can I find the wine shop, please?
– It's on the ground floor.

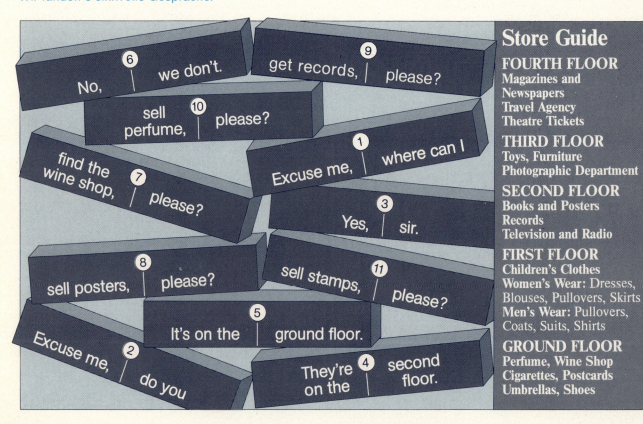

Wortschatzübung

Schreiben Sie, was diese Leute anhaben:

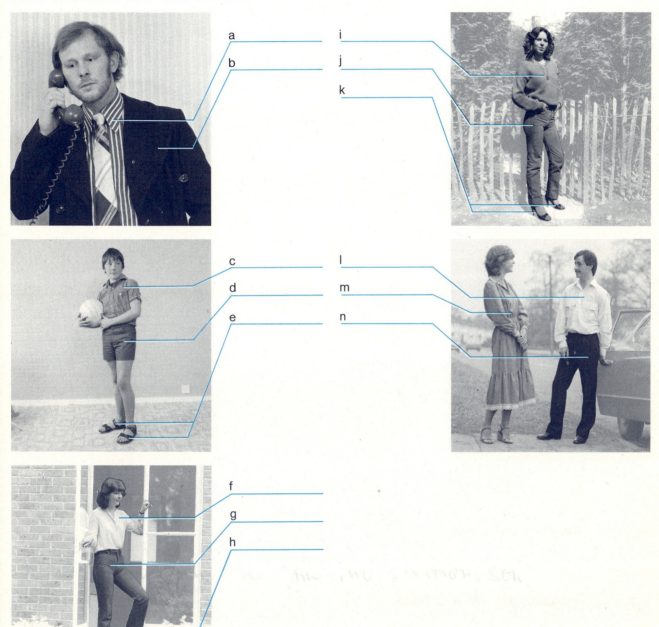

7 Unit

A 2 → A 4

fragen und sagen, ob/wie etwas gefällt:	– What do you think of this red pullover? – It's very nice.
Eigenschaften einer Sache beschreiben (Größe, Preis):	– It's too large./It's not very expensive.
vergleichen:	– Wigton School's cheaper than Kilburn School. – Kilburn School's more modern than Wigton School.

Vergleichen Sie Konfektionsgrößen und Geldbeträge. Ergänzen Sie die folgenden Sätze oder kreuzen Sie das Richtige an.

British and Continental Sizes

WOMEN'S WEAR

Suits, dresses
| British | 10 | 12 | 14 | 16 | 18 | 20 | 22 |
| Continental | 38 | 40 | 42 | 44 | 46 | 48 | 50 |

Shoes
| British | 3 | 4 | 5 | 6 | 7 | 8 | 9 |
| Continental | 35½ | 36½ | 38 | 39½ | 40½ | 42 | 43 |

MEN'S WEAR

Suits, coats
| British | 37–38 | 39–40 | 41–42 | 43–44 |
| Continental | 94–97 | 99–102 | 104–107 | 109–112 |

Shirts
| British | 14 | 14½ | 15 | 15½ | 16 | 16½ | 17 | 17½ |
| Continental | 36 | 37 | 38 | 39–40 | 41 | 42 | 43 | 44 |

Shoes
| British | 7 | 8 | 9 | 10 | 11 | 12 | 13 |
| Continental | 41 | 42 | 43 | 44 | 45½ | 47 | 48 |

a A woman's dress British size 20 is _____ than a Continental one size 38.

b Continental shoes size 38 are _____ than British ones size 6.

c You'd like to buy a shirt in London. Your Continental size is 42. A British size 15½ is ☐ too small ☐ too large for you.

You need a _____ one.

d A man's coat British size 42 is ☐ larger ☐ smaller than a Continental coat size 94.

£1 = about DM 5,–
1p = about 5 Pfennig

e You've got DM 150,– and you'd like to buy a man's suit. But it costs £49; so it's too _____ for you. You need _____ one.

f 'Teacher's' whisky costs about £7 in Britain. That's about DM _____.

In a German supermarket it costs about DM 20,–; so it's _____ than in Britain.

Unit 7

Vergleichen und ergänzen Sie.

Beispiel:
Glasgow: 856,000 people – Edinburgh: 467,000 people

Edinburgh is *smaller than Glasgow*.

a Austria is _____ .

e The trousers _____
_____ the jeans.

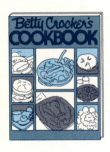 £9.95  £4.95

b 'Betty Crocker's Cookbook' is _____
_____
_____ 'The Vegetarian Cookbook'.

f Many Germans think German beer _____
_____ .

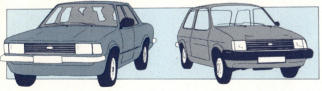

Ford Cortina: £4,110   Austin Metro: £3,157

c An Austin Metro _____
_____ .

g The centre of Frankfurt _____
_____ .

a day – 1450 minutes

d A day _____
_____ .

TV – books/the theatre/concerts: interesting

h Many people think the TV _____
_____ .

Unit 7

B 1 Bitte sehen Sie sich die Anzeige auf Seite 62 genau an und beantworten Sie folgende Fragen.

a Do they sell boys' anoraks at P & J?

   _____ .

b You've got £20. Can you buy a car coat at P & J?

   _____ .

c How much is the tweed car coat?

   _____ .

d Compare the woman's and the man's coat – which is more expensive?

   _____

   _____ . It costs _____ .

e Which is cheaper: the boy's anorak or the girl's coat?

   _____ .

f Do they sell suits for boys and men at P & J?

   _____ .

g How much are the boys' suits?

   _____ .

h Are boys' anoraks cheaper than boys' suits?

   _____ ,

   they are _____ .

B 2 Finden Sie zu jedem Satzanfang (links) eine oder mehrere passende Begründungen (rechts).

1. Jane walks to the office ....

2. Miss Peters goes to town by bus ....

3. Arthur doesn't go to town by car ....

4. Mrs Taylor doesn't walk to the shops ....

5. Mr Lennard doesn't go to work by train ....

6. Cathy goes to her language school by bike ....

a .... because it's more interesting than by bus.

b .... because it's too uncomfortable.

c .... because it's easier by car.

d .... because it's too far.

e .... because it's quicker than the train.

f .... because the tram is too expensive.

7 Unit

sixty-four 64

B 3

1. Ein Makler beschreibt Ihnen am Telefon eine möblierte Wohnung, die er zu vermieten hat. Hören Sie genau zu und tragen Sie auf der hier abgedruckten Liste ein, was die Wohnung zu bieten hat.

```
Check-list
Underground?                              ☐
Train?                                    ☐
Coach?                                    ☐
Kitchen: large                            ☐
         small                            ☐
Bedrooms: 1                               ☐
          2                               ☐
          3                               ☐
Bathroom: with shower/toilet              ☐
          with bath/toilet                ☐
How old?_____
How much?_____ per week
```

2. Vergleichen Sie nun die Grundrisse und Informationen zu einer früher besichtigten Wohnung (Flat 1) und der eben beschriebenen (Flat 2). Bitte kreuzen Sie an, welche der folgenden Feststellungen richtig bzw. falsch sind.

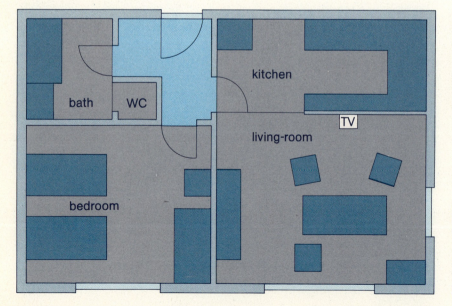

Flat 1

Address: 21 Avendale Road
bedroom, living-room,
kitchen, bathroom
£35 per week
50 minutes from the city centre
two buses
house over 100 years old

Flat 2

B 3

true / false

a You can buy the flats.
b You can rent the flats.
c Both flats have got a living-room, one bedroom, a kitchen and a bathroom.
d Flat 2 has got two bedrooms and two WCs.
e In flat 1 the bathroom is next to the bedroom.
f In flat 2 the living-room is opposite the bathroom.
g Flat 1 is more expensive than flat 2.
h Flat 1 is cheaper because it is older and smaller.
i Flat 2 is nearer to the city centre than flat 1.
j You can take the Underground to the city centre from flat 1.

7 Unit Grammar

1. Plural forms of nouns   Mehrzahlformen von Hauptwörtern (➔ Unit 3.8)

dress – dresses blouse – blouses	[-iz] nach den Zischlauten [s, z, ʃ, ʒ, tʃ, dʒ]

Der Plural von Wörtern, die mit Zischlaut enden, wird auf **-es** gebildet.
Ist schon ein **-e** vorhanden, wird lediglich **-s** angehängt.

child – children [tʃaɪld] ['tʃɪldrən]	man – men [mæn] [men]	woman – women ['wʊmən] ['wɪmɪn]	Einige Hauptwörter bilden die Mehrzahl unregelmäßig.

! Einige Hauptwörter haben nur die Mehrzahlform, z. B.: **jeans, shorts, trousers.**

2. Questions with question words

which?

Which is better – Kilburn School or Wigton School?	Welche (von beiden) ist besser – die Kilburn School oder die Wigton School?

Mit **which?** fragt man gezielt nach einer Sache oder Person aus einer **begrenzten Anzahl.**

how much? – how many?

How much is it? **How many** people walk to work?	Wieviel kostet es? Wieviele Leute laufen zur Arbeit?	**How much?** fragt nach einer Menge: (money) **How many?** fragt nach einer Anzahl: (people)

3. Yes/No questions with **do** and short answers   (➔ Unit 3.1/3.3/3.4)

– **Do**	you	sell	dictionaries?	– Yes, we **do**.	– Führen Sie Wörterbücher? – Ja.
– **Do**	you	sell	stamps, too?	– No, we **don't**.	– Verkaufen Sie auch Briefmarken? – Nein.
auxiliary verb Hilfszeitwort	subject Satzgegenstand	verb Zeitwort	object Ergänzung	short answers	

Grammar Unit 7

4. Negative statements — Verneinte Aussagen

I **don't** go to work by bus. Sorry, I **don't** know.	Ich fahre nicht mit dem Bus zur Arbeit. Ich weiß es leider nicht.

5. have got/has got (→ Unit 5.3)

Have you **got** any black jeans?		
Has it **got** a balcony?	Yes, it **has**.	
	No, it **hasn't**.	

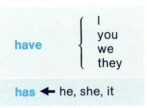

In der 3. Person Einzahl (he, she, it) steht **has** statt **have**.

6. Prop-word: one/ones (→ Unit 4.4)

singular Einzahl	This **coat**'s too large. Have you got a smaller **one**?	Dieser Mantel ist zu groß. Haben Sie einen kleineren?
plural Mehrzahl	These **jeans** are too small. Have you got any larger **ones**?	Diese Jeans sind zu klein. Haben Sie größere?

Soll ein Hauptwort nicht wiederholt werden, so wird es durch **one/ones** ersetzt.
Im Gegensatz zum Deutschen kann das Eigenschaftswort **(larger, smaller)** auch in der Mehrzahl nicht allein stehen.

7. Adjectives: comparison — Eigenschaftswörter: Vergleich/Steigerung

This red pullover's too large. Have you got a small**er** one?
These jeans are too small. Have you got any larg**er** ones?

Eigenschaftswörter mit nur **einer gesprochenen Silbe** bilden die 1. Vergleichsform *(comparative)* durch Anhängen von **-er**.

Kilburn School's **more** modern than Wigton School.
Wigton School's **more** attractive than Kilburn School.

Eigenschaftswörter mit **zwei oder mehr gesprochenen Silben** bilden die 1. Vergleichsform *(comparative)* in der Regel mit **more**.

❗ **good – better** — Einige Eigenschaftswörter bilden die Vergleichsform unregelmäßig.

8. Personal pronouns: subject case – object case (→ Unit 5.6/6.8)

	subject case	object case
– What about these jeans?		
– I like **them**, but **they**'re too large.	they	them

8 Unit

sixty-eight 68

A 1 ↓ A 2

etwas berichten/erzählen und zeitlich einordnen:	– I was at the office till seven (yesterday). – We were at the folk club till about 10.30 (last night).
eine Frage bejahen:	– Yes, he/she was.
eine Frage verneinen:	– No, he/she wasn't.

1. Hören Sie, was Sally einer Freundin am Telefon über den gestrigen Abend erzählt, und beantworten Sie dann folgende Fragen.

a Was Sally at home at six o'clock yesterday evening?

No, _____ , because _____

b Was she at an Italian restaurant after work?

_____.

c Was Sally at the folk club later?

_____ , because _____.

d Where was Sally's friend last night?

_____.

e Where were John and his friends last night?

Perhaps _____.

2. Lesen Sie nun, was Sally am Telefon erzählte, und setzen Sie **was, were** oder **had** in die Textlücken ein.

"Yes, I _____ at the office till seven yesterday. Then I _____ a pizza at an Italian restaurant and after that I _____ three coffees because I _____ so tired.

Where _____ you last night? ...

Oh, you _____ at the folk club! _____ it good? ...

So you _____ a great time yesterday.

_____ John and his friends at the club, too? ...

Oh, perhaps they _____ at John's place then. ...
OK, see you at the club on Saturday evening.
Bye!"

Unit 8

fragen, was jemand gemacht hat:	– Did you watch TV last night?
eine Frage bejahen:	– Yes, I did.
eine Frage verneinen:	– No, I didn't.
etwas berichten/erzählen:	– I watched 'Escape' on BBC 2. – We had a union meeting till half past nine, and then we played billiards at the club.

A 3 ↓ A 4

Beantworten Sie die Fragen und begründen Sie die Antworten.

Beispiele:
Did you watch ITV last night? — No/watch/film/BBC 2
No, I didn't. I watched the film on BBC 2.

Were you at the folk club on Friday? — Yes/want to meet/Sally/there
Yes, I was. I wanted to meet Sally there.

a Did you watch 'Living Legends' on BBC 1 last night? — No/watch/'The Kid'/BBC 2
No, I didn't. I watched the Kid on BBC 2

b Did you play billiards at the club yesterday? — No/be/office/till nine
No, I didn't. I was at the office till nine

c Were you at the club last week? — Yes/have/club meeting/Friday evening
Yes, I was. I had club meeting on Friday evening

d Did you help Jane with her homework today? — No/want to watch/football match/TV
No, I didn't. I wanted to watch the football match on TV

e Were you at home last weekend? — Yes/have guests/Switzerland
Yes, I was. I had guests of Switzerland.

8 Unit

seventy 70

A 5 ↓ A 7

persönliche Informationen erfragen und geben (Lebensdaten):	– Where/When was Charlie Chaplin born? – He was born in London in 1889. – Where/When/What/Why did Chaplin…?
etwas zeitlich einordnen:	– He first appeared in music halls and then… In 1910 he went to the USA… He met his last wife in 1942…

Unit 8

Sir Alfred Hitchcock: 1899–1980

Alfred Joseph Hitchcock was born in London on August 13, 1899. He went to school and university there, and in 1920 he started work with a British film company. In 1920 he also married Alma Revelle, his wife for the next sixty years. They had one daughter.

From 1925 to 1939 he made several films in Britain including 'The 39 Steps' and 'The Man Who Knew Too Much'.

In 1939 he left Britain because he wanted to work in Hollywood. He lived in Los Angeles for the rest of his life and made many of his 53 films there. A lot of people in America and Europe saw Hitchcock's famous films 'Psycho' (1960) and 'The Birds' (1963).

Queen Elizabeth II made Hitchcock 'Sir Alfred' in 1980. Soon after that, in May 1980, he died in Los Angeles.

A 5
↓
A 7

Fragen Sie gezielt nach den unterstrichenen Informationen über Alfred Hitchcock.

Beispiel:
– Alfred Hitchcock was born in London.
– Where was he born?

a He was born on August 13, 1899. — When was he born?

b He went to school and university in London. — Where did he go to school?

c In 1920 Hitchcock started work with a British film company. — What did he do in 1920?

d He made 'The 39 Steps' in Britain. — Where did he make "The 39 Steps"?

e Hitchcock left Britain because he wanted to work in Hollywood. — Why did he leave Britain?

f He made his famous film 'Psycho' in 1960. — What did he make in 1960?

g Elizabeth II made Hitchcock 'Sir Alfred' in 1980. — When did she make him "Sir Alfred"?

h Hitchcock died in Los Angeles in May 1980. — Where did he die in May 1980?

8 Unit

B 1 Im Flugzeug London–Zürich kommen Chris Mayman und Renate Hauser miteinander ins Gespräch. Hören Sie das Gespräch von der Cassette und kreuzen Sie die Sätze an, die die Unterhaltung korrekt wiedergeben.

1. Renate Hauser is on her way back
   a ☐ to England.
   b ☐ to London.
   c ☐ to Germany.
   d ☐ to Zurich.

2. Her neighbour is
   a ☐ Swiss, too.
   b ☐ Scottish.
   c ☐ English.
   d ☐ German.

3. Renate was
   a ☐ on business in Britain.
   b ☐ on holiday in England and Scotland.
   c ☐ on business in London.
   d ☐ on holiday in Switzerland.

4. In London she
   a ☐ visited the Tower and St. Paul's Cathedral.
   b ☐ didn't have a good time.
   c ☐ only stayed for three days.
   d ☐ went to pubs, theatres and concerts.

5. From London she
   a ☐ went to Manchester and Leeds ...
   b ☐ travelled to Edinburgh ...
   c ☐ went to Oxford by car ...
   d ☐ travelled to the Scottish lakes ...

6. ... because she
   a ☐ likes old towns.
   b ☐ wanted to rent a car.
   c ☐ didn't like London.
   d ☐ wanted to visit friends there.

7. After that Renate
   a ☐ went to Manchester.
   b ☐ returned to London.
   c ☐ travelled to Scotland.
   d ☐ went back home.

8. Chris Mayman
   a ☐ is going to Zurich for a holiday.
   b ☐ works for a Swiss import firm.
   c ☐ is going to Zurich on business.
   d ☐ is the general manager of a British firm.

Unit 8

Von der Cassette hören Sie eine heitere Geschichte, die beim Besuch einer Gruppe aus der englischen Stadt Gloucester in der Partnerstadt Trier wirklich passiert ist.
Schreiben Sie in die Lücken die fehlenden Formen der Zeitwörter say, want (x 2), ask, phone, visit, be.

B 2 ↓ B 3

A group of people from Gloucester _____ their twin city Trier and _____ to go to the Trier museum. Their hosts _____ to take them, but the English visitors _____ : "We can find our way."

About an hour later, the visitors _____ their hosts. "Where are you?", the hosts _____ .

"We don't really know," _____ the answer, "but the name of the street is 'Einbahnstraße'!"

Die Vergangenheitsformen der folgenden 23 Zeitwörter haben Sie in Unit 8 gehört, gelesen, gesprochen.
In den vier Wortbaukästen sind die Buchstaben dieser Vergangenheitsformen enthalten. Schreiben Sie diese in die Leerzeilen und streichen Sie die benutzten Buchstaben. In jedem Kasten bleiben einige Buchstaben übrig; daraus können Sie pro Kasten ein Wort bilden. Die vier gefundenen Wörter ergeben dann einen Satz.

B 1 ↓ B 3

a̶ a a a c̶ a̶	a d d d d	a a a d d d d	a a b d d d d
d d d d e e	e e e e g	d e e e e e e	e e e e e e
e e f h̶ h i	i i i l m m	e f i i j l l n	g i i i i l
l l n p r t t	n n o r r s	n n o s r r t t	m n n r s s s
w w w y	t t u v w y	t t t t v v y	t t t u v y

have	had	go _____	leave _____	visit _____
watch _____	sign _____	enjoy _____	make _____
do _____	meet _____	travel _____	result _____
want _____	marry _____	invite _____	say _____
play _____	live _____	attend _____	stay _____
fly _____	die _____	start _____	

_____ _____ _____ _____ ?

8 Unit Grammar

1. Past simple

Das **past simple** wird zur Wiedergabe von Geschehen verwendet, das in der Vergangenheit stattfand und abgeschlossen wurde. Dabei spielt keine Rolle, ob das Geschehen Jahre oder nur eine Minute zurückliegt. Das **past simple** wird oft von einer Zeitbestimmung der Vergangenheit (z. B. **an hour ago; last night; last week; in 1914**) begleitet.

2. Past simple of **be, have** and **do**

- Where **were** you yesterday?
- **Was** John at the pub last night?
- And where **were** Simon and his friends?

- I **was** at the office till seven.
- Yes, he **was**./No, he **wasn't**.
- They **were** at the folk club. And where **were** you last night?

- We **were** at the disco.

be hat im **past simple** zwei Formen:

| I, he, she, it | was |
| we, you, they | were |

Past simple of **have**

- I **had** so much work yesterday evening.
- She **had** a lot of work, too.
- So you **had** a good time?

- And what about Sally?
- That's a shame. We **had** a Chinese meal last night.
- Yes, great!

Das **past simple** von **have** ist in allen Personen Einzahl und Mehrzahl **had.**

Past simple of **do**

- **Did** you watch 'The Kid' on TV last night?
- No, I **didn't**. When was it on?

- **Did** you watch TV last night?
- No, we **didn't**. We had a union meeting.

Charlie Chaplin **didn't** stay with Karno very long.

Das **past simple** von **do** ist in allen Personen Einzahl und Mehrzahl **did.**

3. Past simple of regular verbs   Das past simple der regelmäßigen Zeitwörter

In his second film Chaplin introduc**ed** the little tramp.

- Did you watch 'The Gentle Touch' on ITV last night?
- No, I didn't. I watch**ed** 'Escape' on BBC 2.

- Did you watch 'The Kid' on TV last night?
- No, I want**ed** to see it, but we had a union meeting, and then we play**ed** billiards at the club.

introduce – introduc**ed** [-t]

watch – watch**ed** [-t]

want – want**ed** [ɪd]
play – play**ed** [-d]

Grammar Unit 8

Die regelmäßigen Zeitwörter bilden das **past simple** für alle Personen in Einzahl und Mehrzahl durch Anhängen von **-ed** an die Grundform. Endet die Grundform auf **-e**, wird nur **-d** angehängt.

In 1943 Chaplin marr**ied** Oona O'Neill.

marr**y** – marr**ied**

Zeitwörter, die auf **Mitlaut + y** enden, bilden das **past simple** auf **-ied**.

4. Past simple of irregular verbs
Das past simple der unregelmäßigen Zeitwörter

In 1910 Chaplin **went** to the USA. He **made** his first film in 1914.
In 1952 he **left** the USA for political reasons.

Eine Reihe von Zeitwörtern bilden das **past simple** nicht auf **-ed**. Das **past simple** dieser Zeitwörter unterscheidet sich in Schreibung und Aussprache meist stark von der Grundform, z. B.:

Grundform	go [gəʊ]	make [meɪk]	meet [mi:t]	leave [li:v]	fly [flaɪ]	say [seɪ]	know [nəʊ]	mean [mi:n]	ride [raɪd]
past simple	went [went]	made [meɪd]	met [met]	left [left]	flew [flu:]	said [sed]	knew [nju:]	meant [ment]	rode [rəʊd]

Eine Liste der in ON THE WAY 1 vorkommenden unregelmäßigen Zeitwörter finden Sie auf Seite 136 des Lehrbuchs.

5. Past simple: Summary of verb forms

	be	have	do	regular verbs e.g.: want
singular				
I you he/she/it	was were was	had	did	wanted
plural				
we/you/they	were			

8 Unit Grammar

6. Questions with question words: **when, where** (➜ Unit 3.3/3.4)

- **When** did Chaplin leave the USA?
- In 1952.

- **Where** was Chaplin in 1913?
- In Hollywood.

7. Sentences with adverbials of place and time
Sätze mit Umstandsbestimmungen des Ortes und der Zeit (➜ Unit 5.5)

I was Was he We were	at his place at the pub at the folk club	an hour ago. last night? till ten.	Ich war War er Wir waren	vor einer Stunde gestern abend bis zehn	in seiner Wohnung. in der Kneipe? im Folk Club.
	place Ort	time Zeit		Zeit	Ort

**Folgen Umstandsbestimmungen des Ortes und der Zeit aufeinander, so gilt im Englischen die Faustregel:
Ort vor Zeit.**

8. Personal pronouns object case: **him, her**
(➜ Unit 5.6/6.8/7.8)

Chaplin made his first film in 1914.
In his second film he introduced the little tramp.
This character made **him** famous.
In 1942 he met Oona O'Neil and married **her**
a year later.
She was then 18 years old.

Summary

Personal pronouns:	subject case	object case
singular **1st person**	I	me
plural	we	us
singular **2nd person**	you	you
plural		
singular **3rd person**	he, she, it	him, her, it
plural	they	them

Unit 9

A 1
↓
A 2

etwas bestellen:	– Can I reserve (a table)?
persönliche Informationen erfragen (Name):	– Can I have your name, please?/ What was the name, please?
Gesprächsablauf sichern:	– How do you spell that?
etwas zeitlich einordnen:	– I phoned yesterday.

Von der Cassette hören Sie drei Gespräche:
– Auskunftsgespräch im Kaufhaus;
– telefonische Buchung eines Hotelzimmers;
– telefonische Vorbestellung eines Tisches im Restaurant.

Stoppen Sie die Cassette nach jedem Gespräch und kreuzen Sie die jeweils richtigen Aussagen an.

In a department store

1. The man wants
a ☐ postcards.
b ☐ books.
c ☐ stamps.
d ☐ postcards and stamps.

2. You can get stamps
a ☐ in the store.
b ☐ at the post office.
c ☐ in the store and at the post office.
d ☐ in Baker Street.

Booking a room

1. The woman wants a room
a ☐ for two weeks.
b ☐ from Monday the 19th to Friday the 30th.
c ☐ from Monday the 9th to Friday the 13th.
d ☐ from Sunday the 9th to Friday the 13th.

2. Her name's
a ☐ Maria Maier.
b ☐ Maria Mayer.
c ☐ Maria Meyer.
d ☐ Maria Meier.

Reserving a table

1. The man wants
a ☐ a table for seven for this evening.
b ☐ a table for four for tomorrow evening.
c ☐ a table for eight for this evening.
d ☐ a table for eight for tomorrow evening.

2. At
a ☐ 6.30 p.m.
b ☐ 6.30 a.m.
c ☐ 7.30 a.m.
d ☐ 7.30 p.m.

9 Unit

 Nun hören Sie sich die Gespräche noch einmal an. In jedem kommen zwei Auskunftsfragen mit can vor. Schreiben Sie diese Fragen auf.

In a department store

1. _____?

2. _____?

Booking a room

1. _____?

2. _____?

Reserving a table

1. _____?

2. _____?

A 3

etwas bestellen:	– Waiter, can I/we have the menu, please?
	– Excuse me, Miss, can you bring me/us the wine list?
auf Bestellungen reagieren:	– Yes, sir/madam. I'll bring it right away./Here you are.

Sehen Sie sich dieses Bild genau an. Es zeigt einen für eine Person vollständig gedeckten Tisch im Restaurant.
Vergleichen Sie damit die kleinen Bilder auf der nächsten Seite. Was fehlt?
Bitten Sie den Ober, Ihnen die fehlenden Sachen zu bringen.

79 seventy-nine   **Unit 9**

a  Waiter, _____ ?

b  _____ ?

c  _____ ?

d  _____ ?

e  _____ ?

f _____ ?

A 4

| Wünsche äußern: | – We'd like to order. |
| etwas bestellen: | – I'd like tomato soup (to start with).
– (I think) I'll have the same. |

Ann und Jill essen im Restaurant – aber was bestellen sie?!?

Ann: Waiter, we'd like to order.
I'll have k i n c e c h soup to start with.
Jill: And I'll have m o o t a t juice.
Ann: And to follow I'd like m a l b s c o p h.
Jill: I'll have h t e e a m s.
Ann: And I'd like a cup of e a t. What would you like to drink, Jill?
Jill: I think I'll have d e r i w e n.

Ann:
To start with: _____ soup
To follow: _____
To drink: _____

Jill:
To start with: _____ juice
To follow: _____
To drink: _____

9 Unit

A 5 ↓ A 6

Eigenschaften einer Sache erfragen und beschreiben:	– What's/What are ... like? It's/They're ...
Zufriedenheit/Unzufriedenheit ausdrücken:	– It's very nice./It's not very good./etc.
fragen, ob/wie etwas gefällt:	– Did you enjoy ...?
sagen, ob/wie etwas gefällt:	– Yes, it was excellent.

Jennifers Freund Nick macht drei Wochen Urlaub auf der Insel Jersey; sie schreibt ihm:

June 1st

Dear Nick,

What's Jersey like?! I've got so many questions about your trip! What's the weather like there? And the beach? Is your hotel comfortable? Is the food good? What are the other guests like? Are you enjoying your holidays? I'd love to come and visit you, but I have to work till August. Oh, well, that's life. Please write!

Love,
Jennifer

very	interesting	cold
not very	nice	wet
too	great	expensive
	(un)comfortable	

81　eighty-one　　　　　　　　　　　　　　　　　　　　　　　　　Unit　**9**

1. Nick antwortet Jennifer – er ist nicht sehr zufrieden. Setzen Sie Wörter aus der Worttafel auf S. 80 ein, die seine Unzufriedenheit ausdrücken.

A 5
↓
A 6

> June 8th
>
> Dear Jennifer,
> 　Thanks for your letter. Our flight to Jersey was interesting, but the weather here's _____ _____. My hotel isn't very good: my bed's so _____ I can't sleep, and the food here's _____. The other guests are _____. The beach is great, but we can't go for a swim because the sea's _____.
> 　Only two more weeks, then I'll be home.
> 　　　　　　　　　　　　Love, Nick

2. Nick wechselt das Hotel, das Wetter wird besser – er schreibt nochmals, diesmal begeistert.
Setzen Sie Wörter ein, die Nicks Zufriedenheit ausdrücken.

> June 13th
>
> Dear Jennifer,
> 　Summer is here! Jersey's _____ when the weather's not so _____. I left the Beach Hotel last week and am now at Harrod House. It's _____, and the summer guests here are _____. It's not far from the beach. There's a _____ little pub near here, too.
> 　It's a shame you can't be here, too. See you next week.　Love, Nick

9 Unit

eighty-two 82

A 7
↓
A 8

jemanden nach dem Weg fragen (Verkehrsmittel):	– Does this bus/the 615 go to Dover?/ How do I get to ...?/Which is the bus to ...?
eine Frage bejahen:	– Yes, it does.
eine Frage verneinen:	– No, it doesn't.
Notwendigkeit ausdrücken:	– You want the 615./ (I think you have to) take the 608.

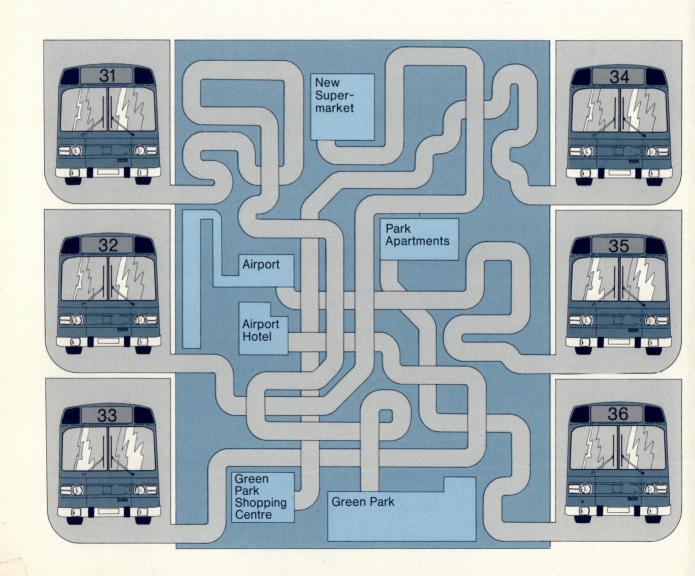

a Does the 31 go to Park Apartments?

_____.

A 7
↓
A 8

b How do I get to the new supermarket?

_____.

c Does the 33 go to the Airport Hotel?

_____.

d Which is the bus to Park Apartments?

_____.

e How do I get to the airport?

_____.

f Which is the bus to the Green Park Shopping Centre?

_____.

Aussprachübung

Suchen Sie für jedes Wort in der linken Spalte reimende Wörter aus der rechten Spalte heraus (es kann mehr als ein Reimwort geben). Schreiben Sie die entsprechenden Wörter in die Leerzeilen und streichen Sie sie in der rechten Spalte.

Hören Sie anschließend die Cassette zur Kontrolle.

a soup: _____

b steak: _____

c peas: *please,* _____

d pie: _____

e toast: _____

f four: _____

g two: _____

group
more
hope
fly
cup
couple
cheese
or
week
I
you
speak
take
like
post
police
goodbye
through
tea
~~please~~
free
go
do
door
hour
buy
now

B 1

9 Unit

eighty-four 84

B 2 Mike und Mary sind übers Wochenende in York, um Freunde zu besuchen und die Stadt anzuschauen. Sie wohnen im Acomb Hotel und wollen von dort überallhin mit dem Bus fahren – aber sie sind immer verschiedener Meinung über die richtige Busroute.
Entscheiden Sie nach der Bus-Streckenkarte, wer jeweils recht hat.

a *Mary:* Nancy and George live in Foxwood Lane. How do we get there?
  Mike: We have to take the 2 to Askham Lane, then change to the 22.
  Mary: I think we can take the 12.

  Who is right?

b *Mary:* Judy Thompson lives in Clifton ... We can take the 2 from here.
  Mike: Oh, I think we have to change to the 19 in the city centre or in Bootham Road.

  Who is right?

c *Mary:* Let's go to the South Bank. We can take the 2, get off at the city centre, and change to the 3 or the 4.
  Mike: I think we have to take the 20 to St Helens Road, and then the 10.

  Who is right?

d *Mike:* Hmm ... How do we get to the city centre?
  Mary: We can take the 2 from here.
  Mike: Oh, no, we can't. We need the 12.

  Who is right?

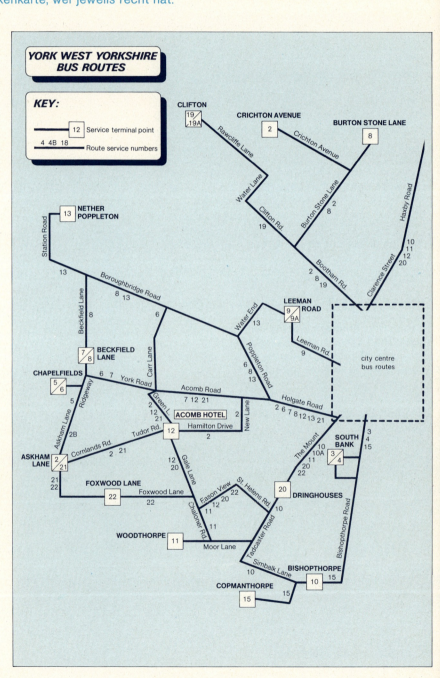

Unit 9

Blackpool ist ein beliebtes englisches Urlaubsziel am Meer. Auf der nächsten Seite werden einige der vielen Hotels angepriesen. Lesen Sie die Anzeigen genau durch und entscheiden Sie, welche Hotels richtig sind für die folgenden Familien:

B 3
▼
B 4

a   Mr and Mrs Clarke want to visit Blackpool for their Christmas holidays. They want a double room with a bath and TV in a hotel with a New Year party.

They can book a room in the

_____ Hotel.

b   The Owen family want to visit Blackpool for their summer holidays. They have three children and a dog.

They can book accommodation in the

_____ Hotel.

Mary Thomas möchte eine Ferienwohnung in Bournemouth buchen. Ergänzen Sie ihren Brief mit den Wörtern aus der Worttafel.

28 Garden Road
Glasgow
Scotland

Seaview Holiday Flats
142 Bodogan Road
Bournemouth BH2 6NQ   15/1/81

Dear Sir/Madam,

I _____ your advertisement _____ the newspaper this morning. I'd like to _____ accommodation _____ three persons (I've _____ two children, ages 5 and 3) _____ Saturday, July 4th _____ Saturday, July 18th.
I'd _____ a flat with two single beds for the children.
I _____ a deposit of £9.

Yours sincerely,
Mary Thomas

enclose	for
got	from
like	in
reserve	to
saw	

Unit 9 Grammar

1. Position of direct and indirect objects — Die Stellung der direkten und indirekten Ergänzungen

Can we	have		the menu,	please?	Können wir		bitte die Speisekarte	haben?
Can you	bring	us	the wine list,	please?	Können Sie uns		bitte die Weinkarte	bringen?
Can you	tell	me	the time,	please?	Können Sie mir		bitte die Uhrzeit	sagen?
	verb	indirect object	direct object					

Folgen einem Zeitwort zwei Ergänzungen, so steht in der Regel die indirekte vor der direkten Ergänzung.

2. have to = müssen

- **Do** I **have to** change?
- Yes, you **have to** get off at Green Park...

- Muß ich umsteigen?
- Ja, Sie müssen in Green Park aussteigen...

Fragesätze mit **have to** werden immer mit einer Form von **do** gebildet.

3. will / 'll

- Miss, can you bring us the menu, please?
- I**'ll** bring it right away.

- Fräulein, können Sie uns bitte die Karte bringen?
- (Ich bringe sie) Sofort.

- I'd like roast beef.
- And I**'ll** have lamb chops.

- Ich hätte gerne Roastbeef.
- Und ich nehme Lammkoteletts.

- I think I**'ll** book flat number 14.

- Ich glaube, ich buche Appartement 14.

Mit Hilfe der **will-form** kann man einen Wunsch oder eine Absicht ausdrücken. Das Deutsche verwendet für diesen Zweck in der Regel die Zeitformen der Gegenwart.

4. Short forms

I**'ll** bring it right away.
We**'d** like to order.
It**'s** got a shower but it**'s** expensive.

I ~~wi~~ll bring it right away.
We ~~woul~~d like to order.
It ~~ha~~s got a shower but it ~~is~~ expensive.

❗ **He's/she's/it's** kann sowohl die Kurzform von **he/she/it is** als auch von **he/she/it has** sein.
Die Bedeutung geht meistens aus dem Zusammenhang hervor.

Grammar Unit 9

5. Possessive pronouns (nominal form): yours — Alleinstehende besitzanzeigende Fürwörter

| What's **your** steak like? – It's very nice, and **yours**? | Wie ist dein/Ihr Steak? – Sehr gut, und deines/Ihres? |

Alleinstehende besitzanzeigende Fürwörter ersetzen ein besitzanzeigendes Fürwort + Hauptwort: **yours** anstatt **your steak.**

6. Adverbials of time — Umstandsbestimmungen der Zeit

yesterday this tomorrow Friday	morning afternoon evening	last night tonight	
		tomorrow Friday	night

"Of course I know what it means. She's hungry."

10 Unit

A 1

> Wünsche äußern: – I'd like to send this letter to Germany./
> I want to send this postcard to Austria.

Eine Gruppe deutscher Touristen reist nach Boston, USA. Jeder sagt, was er unternehmen will. Bitte ergänzen Sie.

Beispiele:
Gudrun Weismüller: "…/want/…/the Boston Tea Party Ship"
"I want to see the Boston Tea Party Ship."

Johanna & Peter Schmitz: "…/like/…/Harvard University"
"We'd like to visit Harvard University."

a Andrea & Georg Scholl: "…/want/…/shopping"

b Günter Braun: "…/want/…/a tour of the city"

c Hedda Meyer: "…/like/…/a tour of the city, too"

d Gabriela & Ludwig Werner: "…/like/…/American friends"

e Ansgar Kohl: "…/want/…/a car and drive to New York City"

A 2

> sich entschuldigen: – I'm sorry.
> (I'm not used to English money yet.)
>
> auf eine Entschuldigung reagieren: – That's all right.

Andreas Müller fährt nach England. Da er sich nicht gut auskennt, kommt er gelegentlich in Situationen, in denen er sich entschuldigen muß.
Ergänzen Sie die Kurzgespräche, indem Sie die Satztafel benutzen.

I'm sorry.	I'm not used to English money yet. I didn't see that.
	That's all right.

Unit 10

Beispiel:

A 2

– No parking here, please; it's not allowed.
– *I'm sorry. I didn't see that.*

– No smoking here, please; it's not allowed.
– I'm _____ .

– Just a moment, that's only 20p. The magazine costs 40p.
– _____
  _____ .
– _____ all right.

– Excuse me, sir, but this table's reserved.
– _____ .
– _____ .

10 Unit

A 3

Sachinformationen erfragen:	– Do you cash traveller's cheques?
Bedauern ausdrücken:	– No, I'm sorry, we don't.
Gesprächsablauf sichern:	– Sorry, I didn't quite understand. Can you repeat that please?

Andreas Müller will in einem britischen Kaufhaus einkaufen, aber er hat sein deutsches Geld noch nicht umgetauscht.
Er spricht mit einer Verkäuferin.
Ergänzen Sie das Gespräch.

– Excuse me, I'd like to buy one of these pullovers. Do you take 'Deutschmarks'?

– Sorry, I _____ .
– Do you take German money?

– No, _____ , we don't. You have to go to a bank.
There's a Barclays in St. Edward's Street, just round the corner on the left.

– Oh, err, can _____ ?
– Yes, there's a bank not far from here. Turn left at the corner – that's St Edward's Street – and Barclays Bank's on your left.
– Thank you.

A 4 → A 5

etwas vorschlagen:	– What about Spain?/Let's go to France instead.
zustimmen/ablehnen:	– That's a good idea./Oh, it's a bit too far.
vergleichen:	– Which is the shortest crossing/the most convenient port? – The shortest crossing's from Calais to Dover./ Ostend's the most convenient port for him.

Unit 10

1. Wortschatzübung: Opposites A4 → A5

Suchen Sie zu jedem Wort der linken Spalte ein Wort mit entgegengesetzter Bedeutung aus der rechten Spalte.

a longest   most expensive

b easiest   smallest

c cheapest   hottest

d coldest   shortest

e largest   newest

f oldest   most difficult

2. Familie Graham ist mit ihren 3 Kindern in Edinburgh im Urlaub. Sie wollen ein Auto mieten, um in die Highlands zu fahren, und schauen sich den Prospekt einer Leihwagenfirma an.
Ergänzen Sie das Gespräch mit Wörtern aus der Worttafel in der passenden Form.

| cheap | easy |
| expensive | large |

Alice: Oh, let's take a Vauxhall Chevette.
Geoff: Why?
Alice: Well, it's the _____ car and the _____ car to park...
Geoff: Well, yes, but we need so much room for the five of us and all our things, I'd prefer a Rover.
It's the _____.
Alice: But Geoff, it's in the _____ _____ group!
Geoff: Well, let's take a Chrysler Sunbeam. It's not too long and not too expensive.
Alice: OK, that's a good idea.

GROUP	TIME PLUS MILEAGE		UNLIMITED MILEAGE				
	1 & 2 Days Only		DAYS				1 Week
	Per Day	Plus Per Mile	3	4	5	6	7
	£	p	£	£	£	£	£
A	5.25	6	33.75	45.00	56.25	64.75	64.75
B	6.25	7	38.25	51.00	63.75	73.50	73.50
C	7.00	8	42.00	56.00	70.00	80.50	80.50
D	9.25	9	54.75	73.00	91.25	98.50	98.50

10 Unit

ninety-four 94

A 6

| etwas vorschlagen: | – Shall we go via Hook of Holland? |
| etwas den Vorzug geben: | – I'd prefer to take the ferry from Ostend to Dover. |

Schauen Sie sich das Gespräch zwischen Alice und Geoff auf Seite 93 noch einmal an.
1. Suchen Sie die zwei Sätze heraus, die let's enthalten und schreiben Sie sie hier auf. Dann schreiben Sie die Vorschläge neu, indem Sie den Ausdruck shall we benutzen.

a _____ let's _____ .

_____ shall we _____ ?

b _____ .

_____ ?

2. Alice: "_____ a Vauxhall Chevette."

Geoff: "_____ a Rover."

A 7

Fähigkeit/Unvermögen ausdrücken:	– Do you speak Dutch?
	– Yes, I do./No, I don't.
etwas nach Art und Weise einordnen:	– I speak it fluently./Not very well.

1. Über 3000 Sprachen gibt es in der Welt, aber 12 Sprachen werden von etwa der Hälfte der Weltbevölkerung gesprochen: Chinesisch, Hindi, Arabisch, Portugiesisch, Bengali, Japanisch, dazu sechs weitere europäische Sprachen. Welche sechs Sprachen sind es, und in welcher Reihenfolge? Können Sie sie erraten?

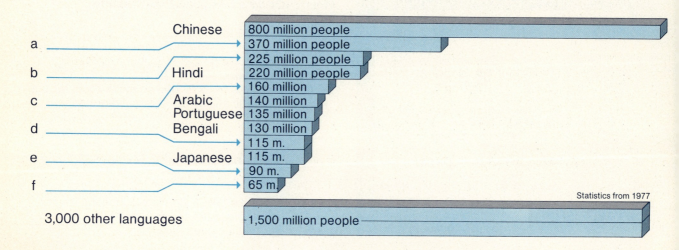

a _____ Chinese — 800 million people
            370 million people
            225 million people
b _____ Hindi — 220 million people
            160 million
c _____ Arabic — 140 million
         Portuguese — 135 million
d _____ Bengali — 130 million
            115 m.
e _____ Japanese — 115 m.
            90 m.
f _____   65 m.

Statistics from 1977

3,000 other languages — 1,500 million people

Unit 10

2. Überall in London können Zeitungsleser (readers) ausländische Zeitungen wie die folgenden kaufen. Beantworten Sie die Fragen.

A 7

Beispiel:

This newspaper comes from Paris.
What language do its readers understand?
They understand English.

a This newspaper comes from Holland.
What language do the people there speak?
_____ .

b Where does this newspaper come from?
It comes _____ .
What language do the people there speak?
_____ .

c Where does this newspaper come from?
_____ Zurich.
Do most people there speak German?
_____ .

d Where does this newspaper come from?
_____ .
What language do the people there speak?
_____ .

e What language do the readers of this newspaper understand?
_____ .

f Does this newspaper come from Germany?
_____ .
Do you speak German?
_____ .

10 Unit

B 1 Auf internationalen Flügen kann man oft zollfreie Waren einkaufen. In den folgenden Gesprächen überlegen sich vier Passagiere, ob sie noch etwas kaufen können oder nicht.
Entscheiden Sie, ob die Meinungen der jeweiligen Gesprächspartner richtig oder falsch sind.

DUTY-FREE ALLOWANCES

TOBACCO GOODS
Cigarettes	200
or	
Cigarillos	100
or	
Cigars	50
or	
Tobacco	250 grams

ALCOHOLIC DRINKS
over 38.8° proof (Whisky, Gin etc.)	1 litre
or	
not over 38.8° proof (Sherry, Port, Champagne etc.)	2 litres
plus	
still table wine	2 litres

true/false

a —Excuse me, can you help me? I'm afraid I don't know the regulations. Can I bring 400 cigarettes with me?
   —Oh, I'm afraid that's far too much. You can only bring 200 duty-free.

b —I'd like to buy two bottles of red wine, but I'm afraid that's too much...
   —What have you got with you?
   —One bottle of Asbach Brandy.
   —Oh, that's not too much then. You can buy the wine.

c —Shall we buy a bottle of Cognac, Ann?
   —Oh, yes. We've only got one litre of wine and a bottle of whisky. That's not too much.

d —Oh, Georgia, let's buy a bottle of whisky.
   —But Jerry, we can't. We've got two bottles of champagne from the duty-free shop in the airport.

97 ninety-seven   **Unit 10**

Die Johnsons planen, was sie am nächsten Sonntag gemeinsam unternehmen wollen. Jeder sagt zuerst, was er selbst tun möchte.

B 2

a Die Bilder zeigen verschiedene Tätigkeiten. Hören Sie die Cassette an. Dann ordnen Sie die Bilder den Familienmitgliedern zu und schreiben die Nummer des entsprechenden Bildes neben den Namen hin. (Einige Bilder bleiben übrig.)

Name	Number
Brian	_____
Ann	_____
David	_____
Ellen	_____
Mrs Johnson	_____
Mr Johnson	_____

b Jetzt sagt jeder noch einmal, etwas langsamer, seinen Vorschlag. Schreiben Sie alle Vorschläge auf.

What do they say?

Brian: _____

Ann: _____

David: _____

Ellen: _____

Mrs Johnson: _____

Mr Johnson: _____

c Welche Wünsche werden in Anns abschließendem Vorschlag berücksichtigt?

_____

(Numbers)

Unit 10 Grammar

1. Adjectives: comparative and superlative forms
(➔ Unit 7.7)

> Let's take the ferry from Ostend to Dover. It's **quicker**.
> Which is the **most expensive** crossing?
> Which is the **easiest** crossing for us?

Eigenschaftswort mit:	einer gesprochenen Silbe		zwei und mehr gesprochenen Silben	zwei Silben, auf -y endend
	quick	short	practical	eas**y**
comparative 1. Vergleichsform	quick**er**	short**er**	**more** practical	eas**ier**
superlative 2. Vergleichsform	quick**est**	short**est**	**most** practical	eas**iest**

Entgegen der Grundregel bilden einige Gruppen von zweisilbigen Eigenschaftswörtern die erste und zweite Vergleichsform durch Anhängen von **-er** bzw. **-est**. Dazu zählen die zweisilbigen Eigenschaftswörter, die auf **-y** enden.

2. what? which?
(➔ Unit 7.2)

– **What** languages do you speak, Carol? – German and Dutch.	– Was für Sprachen sprichst du, Carol? – Deutsch und Holländisch.
– **Which** is the easiest crossing for us?	– Welches ist die günstigste Überfahrt für uns?

Mit **what** fragt man nach einer offenen, unbekannten Menge von Sachen/Personen.
Mit **which** fragt man gezielt nach einer begrenzten, bekannten Menge von Sachen/Personen.

3. Possessive pronouns (nominal form): mine   Alleinstehende besitzanzeigende Fürwörter
(➔ Unit 9.5)

– Which is your luggage? – These two suitcases are **mine**.	– Welches ist Ihr Gepäck? – Diese zwei Koffer sind meine.

4. Adverbs   Umstandswörter

-ly adverbs   Umstandswörter mit der Endung **-ly**

	adjective	adverb
– Do you speak German? – Yes, I speak it **fluently**.	fluent	fluent**ly**
– Oh, I'm **terribly** sorry. I didn't know.	terribl**e**	terrib**ly**

Aus den meisten Eigenschaftswörtern kann durch Anhängen von **-ly** ein Umstandswort gebildet werden. Endet das Eigenschaftswort mit einem nicht gesprochenen **-e**, so entfällt dieses beim Umstandswort.

Irregular forms   Unregelmäßige Formen

	adjective	adverb
– Let's go to Britain next summer. – Yes, that's a **good** idea.	**good**	
– Do you speak Russian? – I understand it, but I don't speak it very **well**.		**well**

5. Short forms

let's ← let us

11 Unit

one hundred 100

A 1 ↓ A 2

nach dem Befinden fragen und darauf reagieren:	– How are you?/How's your wife? – Fine, thanks./She's not very well.
Freude ausdrücken:	– I'm pleased to hear that.
Bedauern/Mitleid ausdrücken:	– I'm sorry to hear that.

Dominoes

Aus den 10 Dominosteinen können durch sinnvolle Aneinanderreihung kurze Gespräche gebildet werden.

Beispiel:
1 – 2 – 3 – 7 – 9
– Hello, Bill. How are you?
– Fine, thanks. And you? How's your cold today?
– Much better, thanks.
– I'm pleased to hear that.

Nun schreiben Sie 4 weitere Gespräche aus jeweils 5–6 Dominosteinen auf ein Blatt Papier. Beginnen Sie immer mit Nr. 1.

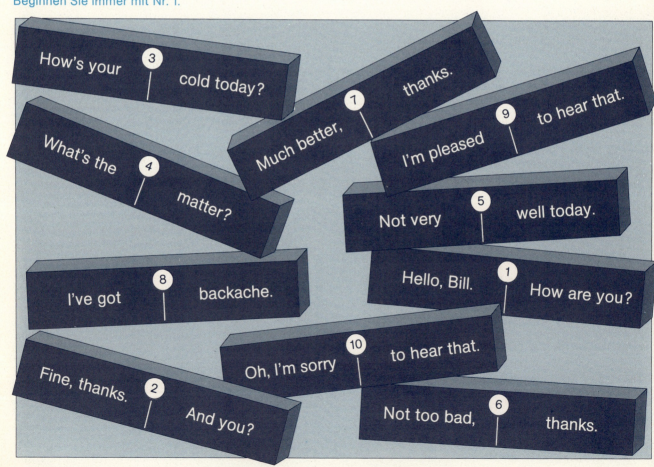

3 How's your | cold today?
7 Much better, | thanks.
9 I'm pleased | to hear that.
4 What's the | matter?
5 Not very | well today.
8 I've got | backache.
1 Hello, Bill. | How are you?
10 Oh, I'm sorry | to hear that.
2 Fine, thanks. | And you?
6 Not too bad, | thanks.

Unit 11

A 3

Ratschläge geben: – Don't drink too much coffee.
It's not good for you.

a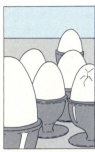

Don't _____
_____ .
You'll get stomach-ache.

d

_____
_____ .
You have to drive home.

b

_____
_____ .
They're very strong.

e

_____
_____ .
It's not good for you.

c

_____
_____ .
It's not good for you.

f

_____
_____ .
You'll be ill.

A 4

etwas vorschlagen (Termin): – Are you doing anything on Tuesday evening?/
Will you be free on Wednesday?/
Will 8 o'clock be all right?

einen Vorschlag annehmen: – Yes, that'll be fine.

einen Vorschlag ablehnen: – I'm afraid I can't come on Tuesday. I'm going to …
No, I won't. I'll be at …

11 Unit

A 4
Ein englischer Bekannter lädt Sie zum Essen ein.
Wählen Sie die jeweils bestgeeignete Antwort und kreuzen Sie sie an.

1. Would you like to come to dinner next week?
   - a ☐ Yes, I'd love to. When?
   - b ☐ Yes, I'd love to. What time?
   - c ☐ Yes, that'll be fine.

2. Well, are you doing anything on Friday?
   - a ☐ No, I can't come on Friday.
   - b ☐ Friday? No, I'm sorry.
   - c ☐ I'm afraid I can't come on Friday. I'm going to a party.

3. Will you be free on Thursday?
   - a ☐ I'm pleased to hear that.
   - b ☐ Yes, fine. What time?
   - c ☐ Fine, and you?

4. Will 7.30 be all right?
   - a ☐ Yes, that'll be fine.
   - b ☐ That's a good idea.
   - c ☐ Yes, that's right.

5. OK. And then you can meet my wife Jill.
   - a ☐ Nice to meet you.
   - b ☐ Great. See you on Thursday then.
   - c ☐ Yes, thanks.

A 4 ↓ A 5

Bedauern ausdrücken:	– No, I'm sorry. I...
etwas zeitlich einordnen:	– I was at the dentist's on Thursday./ I go to my French class on Mondays.

Sally will Jill zum Tee einladen, aber hat Jill Zeit? Hören Sie die Cassette an und notieren Sie Jills Termine im Kalender.

What's Jill doing this week?

October

Sunday 5 — 18th after Trinity

Monday 6 — Week 41

Tuesday 7

Wednesday 8

October

● New Moon — Thursday 9

Friday 10

sr 7.18, ss 6.16 — Saturday 11

October
S M T W T F S
       1 2 3 4
5 6 7 8 9 10 11
12 13 14 15 16 17 18
19 20 21 22 23 24 25
26 27 28 29 30 31

Unit 11

A 6

Zugehörigkeit ausdrücken:	– That's my umbrella./It's mine.
	– Those are your suitcases./They're yours.
sich entschuldigen:	– Oh, I'm sorry. I thought ...

– Excuse me, that's my umbrella.
– Oh, I'm sorry. I thought it was mine.

a
– Excuse me, that's my _____.
– Oh, I'm sorry. I thought it was _____.

d
– Excuse me, those aren't _____.
– Oh, I'm sorry. I thought they were my _____.

b
– Excuse me, those are my _____.
– Oh, I'm sorry. I thought they were _____.

e
– Excuse me, that's my _____.
– Oh, I'm sorry. I thought it was _____.

c
– Excuse me, that isn't _____.
– Oh, I'm sorry. I thought it was my _____.

f
– Excuse me, that isn't _____.
– Oh, I'm sorry. I thought it was my _____.

11 Unit

B 1 **An appointment**

B 2 Während seines Urlaubs an der Küste fühlt sich George Taylor plötzlich sehr unwohl. Er ruft einen Arzt an. Hören Sie, was die Sprechstundenhilfe ihm am Telefon sagt und kreuzen Sie die jeweils beste Erwiderung an.

1. a ☐ Good afternoon. I need a doctor.
   b ☐ Good afternoon. I'd like to make an appointment to see the doctor.
   c ☐ Good afternoon. Can I see the doctor?

2. a ☐ Well, I want to see him.
   b ☐ Oh, but I have to see him. I'm very ill.
   c ☐ No, I can't come on Friday.

3. a ☐ Not too bad, thanks.
   b ☐ My wife's not very well today.
   c ☐ I've got stomach-ache and a terrible headache.

4. a ☐ Yes, that'll be fine.
   b ☐ Yes, I'll be round in five minutes.
   c ☐ Yes, I'd love to.

Hören Sie anschließend das ganze Gespräch zur Kontrolle.

B 4 Bitte schreiben Sie die ausführliche Wettervorhersage für den nächsten Tag fertig. Benutzen Sie dabei diesen Wetterteil aus der Tageszeitung:

Unit 11

Weather forecast for Britain for tomorrow, June 20th   B 4

The south of England and South Wales _____ sunny and _____ with maximum temperatures around 26 degrees Centigrade. London and the Midlands _____ also _____ dry and _____ with temperatures up to 26 degrees Centigrade.

There _____ sunny periods in North Wales, northwest England and the south of Scotland, and it _____ generally _____ with temperatures around 22 degrees Centigrade.

The north of Scotland and Northern Ireland will have sunny intervals with clouds and a little _____ in some places and maximium temperatures around 18 degrees Centigrade.

It _____ much cooler on the coasts with _____ in the east.

ACROSS →
1. "I'd like to make an ... to see the doctor."
6. wet weather
8. "I tried to ... you yesterday, but you weren't at home."
9. The children are ill; they've got terrible ...
11. He has to go to the dentist's. He's got ... ache.
13. pain in the stomach

DOWN ↓
1. People in the USA
2. "Can I ... a window, please?"
3. "How's your husband?" – "I'm afraid he's ... very well."
4. "Don't drink too ... coffee. It's not good for you."
5. phone
7. not well
10. doctor
12. "I go to my French class ... Mondays."

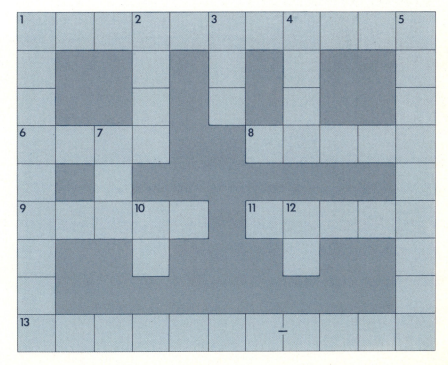

B 1
↓
B 5

11 Unit Grammar

1. to-infinitives   Grundform des Zeitworts mit **to**
(➜ Unit 6.7)

Der **infinitive** mit **to** steht:

a	Nach Eigenschaftswörtern:	I'm **sorry to hear** that. I'm **pleased to hear** that.	Das tut mir (aber) leid! Das freut mich (aber)!
b	Nach Zeitwörtern:	I **tried to phone** you. I **wanted to visit** you.	Ich habe versucht, dich/Sie anzurufen. Ich wollte dich/Sie besuchen.
c	Nach Zeitwörtern + Ergänzung:	I'd like to **make an appointment to see** the doctor.	Ich hätte gerne einen Termin beim Doktor.

2. Negative imperatives   Verneinte Aufforderungs-/Befehlssätze
(➜ Unit 4.6)

Don't drink **Don't** eat	too much coffee. too many green apples.	Trink/Trinken Sie nicht zu viel Kaffee. Iß/Essen Sie nicht zu viele grüne Äpfel.
Don't + Zeitwort in der Grundform	Ergänzung(en) Umstandsbestimmung(en)	Zeitwort (+ Fürwort) + **nicht** + ...

Im Englischen werden Aufforderungs-/Befehlssätze durch vorangestelltes **Don't** verneint.

3. will-future   Ausdruck der Zukunft mit **will** (➜ Unit 9.3)

| – **Will** you **be** free on Wednesday?
– Yes, Wednesday**'ll be** fine.

– **Will** you **be** free on Saturday?
– No, I **won't**.

– I**'ll give** you some tablets. | – Hast du/haben Sie am Mittwoch Zeit?
– Ja, Mittwoch geht.

– Hast du/haben Sie am Samstag Zeit?
– Nein.

– Ich gebe Ihnen Tabletten. | Aufbau des **will-future**:
will/'ll + Zeitwort in der Grundform. |

4. will-future and present continuous (future meaning)
Ausdruck der Zukunft durch **will** bzw. das **present continuous**
(➜ Unit 6.6)

will-future	– **Will you be** free on Monday morning? – No, I **won't**. **I'll be** at the dentist's on Monday morning.	– Hast du/Haben Sie am Montagmorgen Zeit? – Nein. Ich bin am Montagmorgen beim Zahnarzt.
present continuous	– **Are you doing** anything on Tuesday evening? – Oh, I'm afraid I can't come on Tuesday. **I'm going** to the theatre.	– Hast du/Haben Sie am Dienstagabend irgend etwas vor? – Oh, tut mir leid, ich kann nicht am Dienstag. Ich gehe ins Theater.

5. Possessive pronouns (nominal form): mine, yours
(➜ Unit 9.5/10.3)

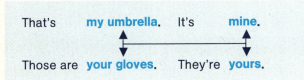

That's **my umbrella**. It's **mine**.
Those are **your gloves**. They're **yours**.

6. much – many
(➜ Unit 7.2)

Don't drink too **much** coffee. Don't take too **many** pills.	Trink nicht zuviel Kaffee. Nimm nicht zu viele Tabletten.

Much steht vor Einzahlwörtern, die eine **nicht zählbare Menge** ausdrücken.
Many steht vor Mehrzahlwörtern, die eine **abzählbare Anzahl** ausdrücken.

7. Short forms

I'll ... ⇐ I ~~will~~ ...
No, I **won't**. No, I **will not**.

12 Unit

one hundred and eight 108

A 1 → A 2

jemanden um Hilfe bitten:	– Can you help me, please?
Notwendigkeit ausdrücken:	– What do I have to do? – You have to ...
etwas zeitlich einordnen:	– First .../then .../after that .../finally ...

In den zwei kurzen Gesprächen werden Anweisungen gegeben. Schauen Sie beim Zuhören die Bilder an und numerieren Sie sie in der richtigen Reihenfolge.

a **At the petrol station**

b **At the Underground station**

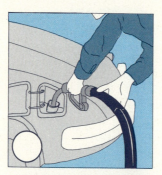

Unit 12

	A 2 ↓ A 3

jemanden um Hilfe bitten und darauf reagieren:	– Can you help me, please?/ Can you check.../look at...? – OK, I'll have a look.
Eigenschaften einer Sache erfragen und beschreiben:	– What's wrong? – There's something wrong with the engine.
jemandem seine Hilfe anbieten:	– Shall I check anything else?

Was sagen die beiden Fahrer zueinander?

12 Unit

A 4

Sachinformationen erfragen und geben:	– Have you checked the battery? – Yes, I have./No, I haven't.
Eigenschaften einer Sache beschreiben:	– It's all right./They're OK.

Bevor John und Mary Fitzpatrick in Urlaub fahren, vergewissern sie sich, ob sie alles erledigt haben.
Ergänzen Sie das Gespräch mit Hilfe der Bilder:

John: Have you phoned your mother? (1)

Mary: No, _____ . I'll do it right away.

Have you _____ all the _____ ? (2)

John: Yes, _____ .

Mary: _____ the _____ ? (3)

John: Yes, and I've _____ , too. (4)

Mary: Oh, good. And have _____ ? (5)

John: Yes, _____ . They're all right.

1  2  3 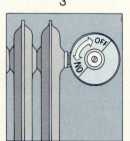 4  5

A 5

Notwendigkeit ausdrücken:	– What do you need for a party? – We'll have to buy some ...
Sachinformationen erfragen (Vorhandensein):	– Have we got any ...?
eine Frage bejahen:	– Yes, we have. There's/There are some left.
eine Frage verneinen:	– No, we haven't. There isn't/There aren't any left.

Unit 12

A 5

Richard kommt von der Arbeit nach Hause und findet eine Nachricht von seiner Freundin Sheila:

> Richard,
> Can you please check what we need for the party? I think there's some beer and wine left from your birthday, but I don't think there's any gin or tonic water. You'll have to buy some.
> And have we got any paper cups and plates left? Please get some if we haven't. I'm afraid we haven't got any fruit juice for Anne and Maggie — you know they don't drink any alcohol. I'll bring some orange juice from the supermarket. I don't think we need any crisps or peanuts, but please check in the kitchen.
> Love, Sheila

Bitte korrigieren Sie Sheilas Vermutungen über ihre Party-Vorräte.

Beispiele:

wine: There _isn't any_ left. They'll have _to buy some_.

paper cups: There _are some_ left. They don't _need any_.

a beer: _____.

b gin: _____.

c tonic water: _____.

d paper plates: _____.

e orange juice: _____.

f crisps: _____.

g peanuts: _____.

A 6

Notwendigkeit ausdrücken:	– We'll have to ...
etwas zeitlich einordnen:	– Have you ... yet? – No, not yet.

> Monday, April 2nd
>
> Dear Jane,
> Thanks for the birthday card. I haven't had time to give a party yet – I've had too much work. But I want to have a party on Saturday. (I'll have to go shopping first because I haven't bought anything to eat and drink yet.)
> I'm going to invite some colleagues from the office – they've sent a card, too. Can you come, too? London isn't very far, and you can stay at my place for the weekend. I'd love to see you again.
> Hoping you haven't made any other plans for the weekend yet,
> Love, Caroline

1. **Beantworten Sie bitte die Fragen mit Kurzantworten.
   (Vorsicht! Nicht alle Antworten werden mit** has **gebildet!)**

a Has Caroline had a lot of work? _____.

b Has she had her birthday party yet? _____.

c Is she going to have the party today? _____.

d Is she going to invite any colleagues? _____.

e Has she invited them yet? _____.

f Can Jane stay at her house on Saturday and Sunday? _____.

Unit **12**

2. Nun kreuzen Sie jeweils true oder false an. Falsche Aussagen korrigieren Sie bitte mit ganzen Sätzen.

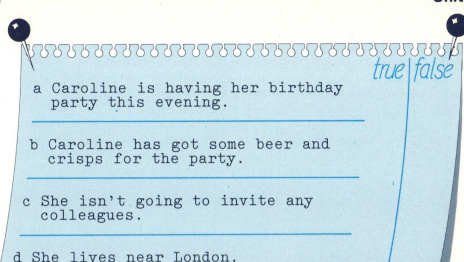

true | false

a Caroline is having her birthday party this evening.
_____

b Caroline has got some beer and crisps for the party.
_____

c She isn't going to invite any colleagues.
_____

d She lives near London.
_____

A 7

etwas anbieten:	– Would you like a ...?
ein Angebot annehmen:	– Yes, I'd love one.
ein Angebot ablehnen:	– No, thank you. I've just had one.

a

– Would you like _____?

– Yes, I'd love one.

b

– Would you like some _____?

– No, thank you. I've _____.

c

– _____?

– Yes, _____.

d

– _____?

– No, thank you. _____ one.

12 Unit

A 7

e – _____
_____ ?
– No, _____ .

f – _____
_____ ?
– Yes, I'd love _____ .

g – _____
_____ ?
– Yes, I'd love one.

h – _____
_____ ?
– No, _____
_____ one.

A 8

jemanden nach seiner Meinung fragen:	– What do you think of Polanski's latest film?
seine Meinung äußern:	– I think it's very good. – I don't think it's very good. – I've never seen any of his films. – I haven't seen it yet.

Stellen Sie sich vor: Einige Gäste aus Großbritannien besuchen Ihren Englischkurs und stellen Fragen. Suchen Sie eine passende Antwort zu jeder Frage und schreiben Sie sie darunter. (Eine Antwort bleibt übrig.)

1. What do you think of English breakfasts?
   _____

2. What do you think of English football teams?
   _____

3. What do you think of ON THE WAY?
   _____

a I don't think it's very good.
b I haven't had any yet.
c I've never seen any of their matches.
d I think it's very good.

Unit 12

Ergänzen Sie die zwei Gespräche zwischen dem Hotelgast John Smith und verschiedenen Hotelangestellten. Schreiben Sie in jede Lücke ein Wort aus der entsprechenden Worttafel.

B 1

– Good evening.
– Hello, this is John Smith in room 22. I think there's something _____ with my shower. Can you come and _____ it, please?
– Certainly, sir. I'll _____ our assistant manager. He'll _____ up to your room right away. Can I help you with _____ else?
– No, thank you.

– You've got _____ with your shower, sir?
– Yes, there isn't _____ water.
– Oh, I'll have a _____ . ... Hmm. Yes, there's _____ wrong with it. I'm afraid we can't _____ it at the moment. I'm terribly _____ , but you'll _____ take _____ room.

another	check	anything
any	come	look
sorry	have to	something
wrong	repair	trouble
	tell	

12 Unit

B 2 → B 3

What do you think has happened?

1.
a ☐ The garage has sent the bill for the car repairs.
b ☐ Someone has sent her money.
c ☐ A friend has invited her to a party.

3.
a ☐ The ambulance has arrived.
b ☐ There has been a road accident.
c ☐ They have just bought a new car.

2.
a ☐ The children have crossed the street on their way to school.
b ☐ There has been an accident at the zebra crossing.
c ☐ The children have just crossed the street on their way home.

4.
a ☐ The dog has eaten the newspaper.
b ☐ The newspaper has just arrived.
c ☐ The woman has read the newspaper.

B 1 → B 4 Sehen Sie sich die Bilder von einer Party auf Seite 117 an, und suchen Sie von unten einen passenden Text zu jeder leeren Sprechblase.

1. a ☐ Yes, and I'll be at the doctor's.
   b ☐ Yes, and I'll call the police.

2. a ☐ We'll just have to go there by train.
   b ☐ I think we'll have to buy a new battery.

3. a ☐ Oh, he's had too much to drink again. He's going to have a terrible headache tomorrow.
   b ☐ He'll have to go to the dentist's tomorrow.

4. a ☐ I haven't seen it yet. Is it good?
   b ☐ I haven't got an invitation.

5. a ☐ I'm sorry to hear that. But come in and have a drink.
   b ☐ Has it just happened?

6. a ☐ No, thank you. I haven't had any yet.
   b ☐ Yes, please. This wine is very good.

7. a ☐ No, never. Have you?
   b ☐ Yes, I often drink champagne.

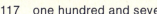

Unit 12 Grammar

1. Past participle
Mittelwort der Vergangenheit

Regular verbs

infinitive	past simple = past participle
repair dial check	repaired dialled checked
invite	invited

Die regelmäßigen Zeitwörter bilden ihre **past simple**- und **past participle**-Form durch Anhängen von **-ed** an die Grundform.

Irregular verbs

infinitive	past simple	past participle
send [send] speak [spi:k] buy [baɪ]	sent [sent] spoke [spəʊk] bought [bɔ:t]	sent [sent] spoken ['spəʊkən] bought [bɔ:t]
put [pʊt] make [meɪk] have [hæv] see [si:]	put [pʊt] made [meɪd] had [hæd] saw [sɔ:]	put [pʊt] made [meɪd] had [hæd] seen [si:n]

Past simple und **past participle** der unregelmäßigen Zeitwörter unterscheiden sich in Schreibung und Aussprache oft stark von der Grundform und voneinander (vgl. Lehrbuch, Seite 136).

2. Present perfect: form

statements:	**I've** never **read** any of Graham Greene's novels. There **has been** another accident at Chapley Corner. Oh, I **haven't seen** it yet.
questions:	**Have** you **checked** the battery? What do you think **has happened**?
short answers:	Yes, I **have**./No, I **have**n't.

Aufbau: **have/has + past participle**
Beispiel: **have checked**

Present perfect: use — Gebrauch

a In der Vergangenheit abgelaufene Handlungen/Vorgänge mit Folgen oder Nachwirkungen in der Gegenwart:

– **Have** you **checked** the battery? — Yes, I **have**.

– **Have** you **repaired** the brake-lights? — No, I **have**n't.

– Would you like a drink? — No, thank you. I've just **had** one.

Grammar Unit 12

b Handlungen/Vorgänge/Zustände, die in der Vergangenheit begannen und in der Gegenwart noch andauern:

We **have written** to the Council several times, but they **have done** nothing. Now we think the time **has come** for action.

– What do you think of Fassbinder's latest film? – Oh, I **have**n't **seen** it **yet**.

Häufige ‚Signalwörter' für den Gebrauch des **present perfect** sind **just, yet, already**.
Das **present perfect** kann grundsätzlich nicht zusammen mit Zeitbestimmungen der Vergangenheit, z. B. **last year, an hour ago**, benutzt werden.

3. Indefinite pronouns: some – any/something – anything
Unbestimmte Fürwörter

Fragesatz: **any, anything**	Verneinter Aussagesatz: **any, anything**	Bejahter Aussagesatz: **some, something**
Have we got **any** wine? Shall I check **anything** else?	No, there isn't **any** left. I don't think there's **anything** wrong with the car.	Yes, there's **some** left from the party. Yes, there's **something** wrong with the engine.

Some/something stehen in der Regel im bejahten Aussagesatz, **any/anything** dagegen in verneinten Aussagesätzen und in Fragesätzen.

4. Adverbs of frequency: position
Umstandswörter der Häufigkeit: Stellung im Satz

Has your teacher	ever		spoken	English in class?	Hat Euer/Ihr Lehrer	jemals	Englisch im Unterricht gesprochen?
He	always often sometimes never		speaks	English in class.	Er spricht	immer oft manchmal nie	Englisch im Unterricht.
	Umstandswort		Zeitwort	Ergänzung(en)/ Umstands- angabe(n)		Umstands- wort	Ergänzung/ Umstands- angabe (+ Zeitwort)

Im Englischen stehen Umstandswörter der Häufigkeit in der Regel **vor** dem Zeitwort.

13 Unit

A 1 ↓ A 2

Zugehörigkeit ausdrücken:
– Have they bought anything for Susan?
– Yes, they've bought her a skirt.

etwas zeitlich einordnen:
– Have you been to the sales yet?
– Yes, I have. I went ... yesterday.

Liz und Jean unterhalten sich am Telefon über ihre Einkäufe. Hören Sie zu und lösen Sie dann die true/false Aufgaben.

true/false

a Liz lives in Shrewsbury.

b Jean has just been shopping.

c Liz is going to town with David next Saturday.

d Liz and David bought some clothes for their daughter.

e They bought her some shoes, too.

f They didn't buy anything for the baby.

g Liz bought a raincoat at Evans's.

h Liz and Jean will be at the meeting on Friday.

A 3

Eigenschaften einer Sache erfragen und beschreiben:
– What was it like?
– It was quite good.

Zufriedenheit/Unzufriedenheit ausdrücken:
– We liked it/didn't like it.

Gundula, die gerade ihren Urlaub in London verbringt, fragt ihre englische Bekannte Betty nach verschiedenen Restaurants. Schreiben Sie unter die im Gespräch unterstrichenen Ausdrücke gleichbedeutende Ausdrücke aus dem Wortkasten auf Seite 121.

Gundula: London's great! We were at the British Museum today. We want to go to a good restaurant tonight. There's a list of restaurants in our guide. – Have you ever been to Leith's?
Betty: Yes, I have.
Gundula: What was it like?
Betty: It <u>was quite good</u>.

Gundula: What about Wheeler's?

Unit 13

A 3

Betty: Yes, we were there a couple of weeks ago.
It <u>was excellent</u>.

My fish dinner <u>was very nice</u>, and Tim liked his meal, too.

You'll need to reserve a table there.
Gundula: Then perhaps we'll try to reserve a table for tomorrow.
Have you ever tried Flanagan's?
Betty: Yes, but don't go there. We went there last Saturday.
It <u>wasn't very good</u>; the food was cold. We didn't like it.

| was very good | wasn't bad |
| wasn't very nice | was very good |

A 3 ↓ A 4

| auf Äußerungen aufmerksam machen: | – By the way, ... |
| persönliche Informationen erfragen und geben: | – Have you heard anything from ...?/Has he ... yet?
– Yes, I have./Yes, he has. |

Programme **VISIT TO EDINBURGH**

Monday, 2nd May	– fly Frankfurt – London – Edinburgh
	– tour of Edinburgh – theatre
Tuesday, 3rd May	– visit to Edinburgh Castle – afternoon free – pub tour
Wednesday, 4th May	– tour of the Highlands
Thursday, 5th May	– free for shopping – fly Edinburgh – London – Frankfurt

<u>price</u>: 435 Marks

a Jessica möchte Edinburgh besuchen. Sie hat sich ein Programm besorgt und versucht jetzt, Elizabeth zum Mitmachen zu bewegen. Ergänzen Sie das Gespräch auf Seite 122 mit den Zeitwörtern aus dem Wortkasten. (Es fehlt jeweils nur ein Wort.)

13 Unit

A 3 → A 4

| been | ~~flew~~ | flown | have | haven't |
| haven't | seen | visited | went |

J.: Look at the programme. It's very interesting.
E.: But I don't like tours, Jessica.
J.: But have you ever flown?

E.: Yes, sure, I _____flew_____ to Chicago last year.

J.: Well, I've never _____, but I'd like to. Have you ever been to Edinburgh?

E.: No, I've never _____ Edinburgh, but I've been to Glasgow.
    I didn't like it. It was too cold.
J.: So you haven't visited Edinburgh Castle yet?

E.: No, I _____. I've never _____ any castles.
J.: And have you ever been on a pub tour?

E.: Yes, I _____. David and I _____ on a pub tour in London
    a couple of weeks ago.
J.: But London isn't Edinburgh! It's different there.

    Have you ever _____ on a tour of the Highlands?

E.: No, I _____. I'm afraid I just don't like tours, Jessica.
J.: That's a shame. It's not very expensive. I think I'll try it.

**b Am Dienstag ruft Jessica aus Edinburgh bei Elizabeth an.
     Ergänzen Sie das Gespräch.**

E.: Well, you wanted to fly. What was it like?
J.: It wasn't bad.

E.: And what _____ the tour of the city like?

J.: It _____ very interesting. And I _____ a lot of souvenirs on the way.
E.: Was the theatre good?

J.: Yes, it _____ excellent.

E.: _____ Edinburgh Castle _____?
J.: Oh, I liked it; it's very old – and cold!

E.: And _____ the pub tour _____?

J.: We haven't _____ on the pub tour yet. It starts at 8 o'clock tonight.
    By the way, have you got my postcard yet?

    I _____ it yesterday.

E.: No, I _____. Perhaps it'll come tomorrow.

A 5

| vergleichen: | – 'Oliver' is one of the best musicals ever. |

In den folgenden sechs Werbeslogans ist immer ein Ausdruck unpassend; streichen Sie ihn durch.

a This is the best/most entertaining/smallest musical ever.
b They are the world's finest/most difficult/most successful dancers.
c His latest book is his longest/most controversial/most comfortable ever.
d It's the greatest/easiest/funniest film this year.
e Go to the Theatre Royal for a most attractive/most entertaining/most unsuccessful evening.
f This restaurant has got the happiest/nicest/biggest steaks in town.

A 6

fragen, ob/wie etwas gefällt:	– Did you like it?/How did you like it?
sagen, ob/wie etwas gefällt:	– (Yes, I did.) I love comedies./I thought it was excellent.
zustimmen:	– So do I./So did I.

Dominoes

Bilden Sie vier kurze Gespräche, indem Sie jeweils mehrere Dominosteine zu einer sinnvollen Reihenfolge zusammensetzen, und schreiben Sie diese Gespräche auf ein Blatt Papier. Beginnen Sie immer mit Nummer 1. Sie können jeden Stein beliebig oft verwenden.

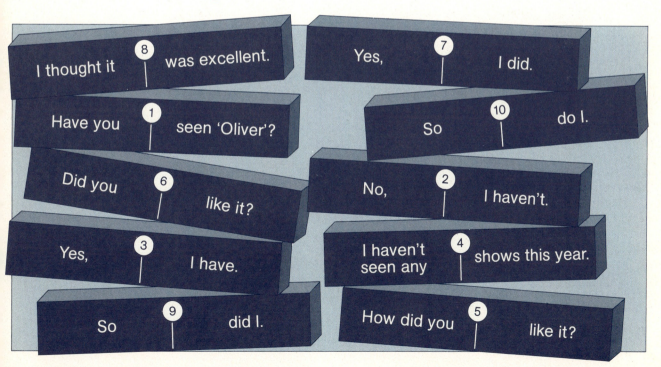

13 Unit

B 1 Helen Baxter-Smith schreibt einen Bewerbungsbrief auf ein Stellenangebot in ihrer Tageszeitung:

```
                                          59 Highfield Road
                                          Tring
                                          Hertfordshire
                                          HP23 4D5

                                          20 May 1981

International Schoolbooks Ltd.
165 Old Brompton Road
London
SW5 0AN

Dear Sirs,

I was very interested to read your advertisement in today's
'Daily Telegraph' and would very much like to hear more about
the sales job you offer.

I was born in St Albans, Herts, on 27 March 1953 and went to
primary and grammar school there. In 1969 I took five sub-
jects at 'O' Level: English language, German, French, Mathe-
matics and Geography.

After that I left school and went to work with Cook's, the
international travel agency, in London. Most of the time there
I organized and sold tours to and from Europe and Africa.

In 1976 I married Peter Smith, who works as an engineer
in Watford. In 1977 I left Cook's and we went to live in
Tring, Herts.

A few months later I found a job with a small firm in Tring
that exports English wines and imports Continental wines.
I wrote most of their letters and made all their phone-calls
abroad till 1979. I have been the firm's export manager for
the past two years.

I think that my qualifications and professional experience
are right for the job you offer. I would really like to work
in London again, and I have always loved books! Please send me
further information about the job or phone me at Tring 3841.

                                          Yours sincerely,

                                          Helen Baxter

                                          Helen Baxter-Smith
```

Unit 13

B 1

1. Der Personalchef von International Schoolbooks Ltd hat Helens Brief gelesen und berichtet dem Sales Manager über Informationen und Eindrücke aus diesem Brief. Beurteilen Sie diese Aussagen:

true / false

a "Mrs Baxter lives in St Albans."

b "She left school at the age of sixteen."

c "Mrs Baxter took four languages at 'O' Level."

d "Her first job was with a wine export/import firm."

e "She left Cook's when she married her husband."

f "Mrs Baxter can write letters and make phone-calls in three languages."

g "She's got no sales experience with books."

2. Beantworten Sie folgende Fragen zu Ihrem eigenen Lebenslauf (soweit sie Sie betreffen). Bitte schreiben Sie ganze Sätze.

a Where and when were you born?

b Where and from when till when did you go to school?

c When did you leave school (month and year)?

d What was your first job?

e Did/Do you like it?

f What is your job now?

g Do you like it?

13 Unit

B 3 Lesen Sie den Zeitungsartikel im Lehrbuch (B 3, Seite 113) noch einmal durch. Dann kreuzen Sie true für die richtigen Sätze und false für die falschen an. Falsche Sätze korrigieren Sie bitte.

true | false

a Mr Fat drank beer every day.

b Mrs Fat liked gin and tonic.

c Fred Fat preferred milk.

d They have never tried to slim.

e The Fat Family now drinks water.

f Water is an expensive drink.

g Water is a dull drink.

B 1 Word Game: Pyramids

↓

B 3 Jedes zweite, dritte bzw. vierte Wort besteht aus den Buchstaben des darüberstehenden Wortes und einem zusätzlichen Buchstaben.

Beispiel:

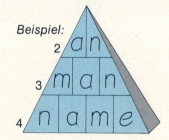

a
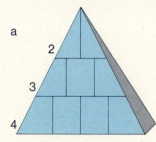

2 Turn ... the tap.
3 doesn't = does ...
4 city

b
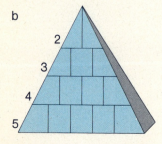

2 An easy way ... slim: try water!
3 A ... of yogurt costs 8½ p.
4 ... the ball!
5 Football is a very popular ... .

c
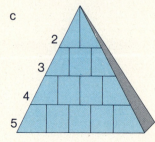

2 I wasn't ... home yesterday.
3 ... and drink
4 What subjects did he ...?
5 beef

Grammar Unit 13

1. Verb + direct object + indirect object   Zeitwort + direkte Ergänzung + indirekte Ergänzung
(➔ Unit 9.1)

	verb	direct object	to/for + indirect object	
Now you Have they	write bought	a letter anything	to Ian Thomas. for Susan?	
Yes, they've Can you	bought tell	her me	a skirt. the time,	please?
	verb	indirect object	direct object	

Bestimmten Zeitwörtern wie **buy, write, bring, tell** können zwei Ergänzungen folgen.
Indirekte Ergänzungen mit **to** oder **for** stehen **nach** der direkten Ergänzung.

2. Present perfect and past simple: use
(➔ Units 8.1/8.2/12.3)

– **Have** you been to the sales **yet**?

– Yes, I **have**. I **went** to town with my husband **yesterday**.

– And **did** you buy anything?

– Waren Sie schon beim Schlußverkauf?/
Sind Sie schon beim Schlußverkauf gewesen?

– Ja. Ich bin gestern mit meinem Mann
in die Stadt gefahren.

– Und haben Sie etwas gekauft?

Der richtige Gebrauch einer der beiden Zeitformen wird im Englischen häufig durch **Signalwörter** und den **Textzusammenhang** bestimmt.

Das **past simple** stellt in der Vergangenheit abgeschlossenes Geschehen dar. Typische **Signalwörter** sind deshalb Zeitangaben der Vergangenheit, z. B.: **last night, yesterday, last week, in 1964**. (➔ Unit 8).
Das **present perfect** stellt Geschehen dar, das in der Vergangenheit begonnen hat, aber entweder noch andauert oder Wirkungen auf die Gegenwart hat, also noch „aktuell" ist. Typische **Signalwörter** sind deshalb **yet, just, already**. (➔ Unit 12.2)

3. Short answers: So do I./So did I.

– I **think**, 'IPI Tombi' 's
the best musical in town.
– **So do I**.

– Ich finde, „IPI Tombi" ist das beste
Musical, das z. Zt. hier läuft.
– Ich auch.

– I **thought** it was excellent.
– **So did I**.

– Ich fand, es war hervorragend!
– Ich auch.

Zur Bestätigung einer positiven Aussage verwendet man im Englischen oft die Konstruktion **so** + Hilfszeitwort + persönliches Fürwort, z. B. **So do/did I**.

14 Unit

A 1 → A 2

sagen ob/wie etwas gefällt und dies begründen:	– He liked it very much./I didn't like it because.../ The children loved it because...
ablehnen/zustimmen:	– Peter was against the idea.../... finally agreed.
etwas nach Art und Weise einordnen:	– ... simply too small/... really cheap/... absolutely beautiful
Fähigkeit ausdrücken:	– Who can repair the roof? – I can do it myself./It's too difficult for me.

Lesen Sie den Brief im Lehrbuch (S. 114) noch einmal durch. Dann kreuzen Sie **true** oder **false** bei den folgenden Aussagen an. Falsche Aussagen korrigieren Sie bitte auf der Leerzeile.

true/false

a Peter and Kathy's old flat is simply too small for their family.

b The modern 3-bedroomed flat was a long way from their old one.

c The modern flat was quite near Peter's office.

d Kathy liked the modern flat because it was on a quiet road.

e The cottage was expensive.

f Kathy and the children didn't like it at first.

g The children can play in the big garden.

h Peter was so enthusiastic that Kathy finally agreed.

i They only have to renovate the kitchen.

j Some of their friends can help them.

Unit 14

A 3

| eine Absicht äußern: | – We're going to buy a cottage./
We're going to renovate it. |

THE MR MEN by Roger Hargreaves

What's the cloud going to do? – It's _____.

A 2
+
A 4

Fähigkeit ausdrücken:	– I can do it myself./ You can't do that yourself.
sagen ob/wie etwas gefällt:	– I really like it./I didn't like it at all.
zustimmen/ablehnen:	– So do I./So did I. Neither do I./Neither did I.
Eigenschaften einer Sache beschreiben:	– It looks nice.

Suchen Sie die richtigen Antworten im folgenden Gespräch aus:

1. *Tim:* Have you seen the children's bedroom?
   Ann: a ☐ Yes, I did.
   b ☐ Yes, I have.
   c ☐ Yes, it does.

2. *Ann:* Did you paint it yourself, Tim?
   Tim: a ☐ No, the children did it.
   b ☐ No, I haven't.
   c ☐ No, I can do it myself.

3. *Ann:* Really? It looks very nice. I like green very much.
   Tim: So do I. But I don't like the curtains very much.
   Ann: a ☐ So did I.
   b ☐ Neither do I.
   c ☐ I don't.

14 Unit

A 5

Zugehörigkeit ausdrücken:
- Here's my suitcase.
- And your parents' luggage?
- Theirs is still in the car.

Ein Hotelangestellter sucht den Besitzer eines Schlüsselbundes unter den anwesenden Gästen. Setzen Sie die fehlenden Wörter ein:

a

- Excuse me, are these your keys, sir?
- No, they aren't _____.

Perhaps they're _____.

b

- Excuse me, are these _____ keys?
- No, they aren't _____.

Perhaps one of the young men over there has lost them.

c

- Excuse me, gentlemen, ...
- Oh, _____ keys! I've forgotten them again, I see. Thank you.

14 Unit

one hundred and thirty-two 132

A 7

Orts-/Richtungsangaben machen: – After you go through the entrance...,
you see the garden centre on your right.

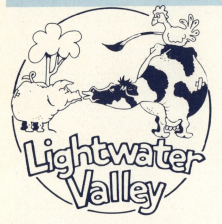

Schauen Sie die Karte von Lightwater Valley im Lehrbuch (S. 120) nochmals an, und hören Sie die Cassette. Sie hören eine Lautsprecherdurchsage über einen kleinen Jungen, der seine Eltern sucht.

a Where did they find the little boy?
   (Markieren Sie die Stelle auf der Karte.)

b Where can his parents find him now?
   _____

B 1
↓
B 2

Linda und Sally, zwei Amerikanerinnen, suchen Arbeit.
Linda ist Hausfrau; sie will nicht ganztags sondern 'part-time' (stundenweise, teilzeit) arbeiten. Sally, bis jetzt Sekretärin, sucht eine neue Ganztagsstelle.
Linda und Sally schauen sich die Stellenangebote ('Help Wanted') in der Zeitung an.
Welche Angebote könnten Linda bzw. Sally interessieren?

Linda:
21 years old, housewife,
loves children; can drive
and has got a car;
has never worked in an office
(can't type*); wants
a part-time job

Sally:
20 years old; loves to drive
and has got a car;
has worked as a secretary for
two years and doesn't like
the job; wants a different
sort of job

* type = Schreibmaschine schreiben

job numbers: _____   job numbers: _____

PAGE TEN-A — Help Wanted

Can you type? Would you like to work part-time?

We are a busy architectural office in Cambridge in need of a first-class typist with 3-5 years experience who can work part-time.

Our needs change constantly and the person we are looking for will be able to work a flexible schedule averaging about 20 hours per week. We expect that you will be needed on a regular basis, however there may be times that you won't work at all.

We are offering $5.00 to $7.00 per hour, depending upon your experience, and we will guarantee you an annual salary, if you can help us with our varied work loads.

Your skill should also include telephone and general office duties.

If this sounds like something you would like, please call Ann at Arrowstreet Inc., 14 Arrow Street, Cambridge, 868-1804, for more information and an appointment. ①

WORK FROM HOME, 3 hrs per day, 5 days per week aver. earn. $100. Call Stanley Home Prod, 623-7475. O,B ②

DRIVERS WANTED

Male and Female. Monday to Friday, 9 AM to 5 PM.

GREEN'S TAXIS

33 Kensington Ave. Somerville, MA ③

PART-TIME HELP WANTED

CAN YOU WORK WITHOUT HELP?
CAN YOU WORK WITH A SMALL GROUP OF TEENAGERS?
CAN YOU WORK 2 TO 3 AFTERNOONS PER WEEK?
WOULD YOU LIKE TO EARN EXTRA MONEY?
HAVE YOU GOT A CAR?
YES?
THEN . . .
WE CAN USE YOU
Call 625-6300 ④

PART-TIME SECRETARY
Cambridge. Hours 8:30 to 12:30, Monday-Friday. Typing, filing, light bookkeeping, some customer contact.
Call Jan at **491-4995** ⑤

Restaurant
WAITRESSES — M/F
Very fast coffee shop exp a must.
Apply after 3PM Greentrees, 42 W. 50 St., NYC ⑥

TYPIST
Excellent salary, all company benefits.
For more information, call Mr. Nasr at
492-2800
BLUE BELL PLASTIC INC.
88 Charles St. Located between Lechmere and Kendall Street ⑦

ASSISTANT SECRETARY
For Cambridge Architect 20-25 hrs. per week. 661-3812 O,B ⑧

ELECTRICIAN
Licensed electrician Monday thru Friday 8 – 4:30 PM
Call 321-3041. ⑨

14 Unit

B 3 Wenn Sie Ihre 'End of Book One Party' vorbereiten, brauchen Sie dringend die Sachen, die Sie hier abgebildet sehen. Lösen Sie damit das Kreuzworträtsel – und Sie haben dieses Arbeitsbuch „hinter sich"!
In der senkrechten Säule können Sie am Schluß einen Ausdruck lesen, der für Ihr Englischlernen wichtig ist.

Meine Lösung: _____

Grammar Unit 14

1. Adverbs: function Umstandswörter: Funktion
(➜ Unit 10.4)

I **really** like it.	verb Zeitwort
I thought it looked **quite** nice.	adjective Eigenschaftswort
Do you speak Spanish? – Not **very** well.	adverb Umstandswort
Luckily several friends have offered to help us.	clause Satz

Umstandswörter können sich auf Zeitwörter, Eigenschaftswörter, andere Umstandswörter oder einen ganzen Satz beziehen.
Dabei verändern sie die Bedeutung dieser Wörter/Sätze, z. B. verstärken sie diese oder schwächen sie ab.

2. Questions with question words: **who?**

Who can repair the roof?	Wer kann das Dach reparieren?
Who can we ask to paint the walls?	Wen können wir bitten, die Wände zu streichen?

Who wird als Satzgegenstand (wer?), aber auch als Ergänzung (wen?) verwendet.

3. **be going to**-future
(➜ Units 6.6/11.3/11.4)

– We're **going to buy** a cottage. It's quite old but we're **going to renovate** it.	– Wir wollen ein Häuschen kaufen. Es ist ziemlich alt, aber wir werden es renovieren.
– What **are** you **going to do**? **Are** you **going to renovate** it yourselves?	– Was wollt ihr machen? Wollt ihr es selbst renovieren?

Aufbau: Form von **be + going to + Grundform** eines Zeitworts

Mit dem **be going to-future** drückt man aus, daß ein zukünftiges Geschehen erwartet wird bzw. eine Handlung beabsichtigt ist.

14 Unit Grammar

4. Reflexive pronouns: myself, yourself, ourselves, yourselves
Rückbezügliche Fürwörter

– Who can repair the roof? – I think I can do it **myself**. – No, you can't do that **yourself**!	– Wer kann das Dach reparieren? – Ich glaube, das kann ich selbst machen. – Nein, das kannst du nicht selbst!
– We've papered the lounge **ourselves**. – Are you going to paper the other rooms **yourselves**, too?	– Wir haben das Wohnzimmer selbst tapeziert. – Wollt ihr die anderen Zimmer auch selbst tapezieren?

Während es im Deutschen nur das Wort **selbst** für alle Personen gibt, hat das Englische für jede Person in Einzahl und Mehrzahl ein eigenes rückbezügliches Fürwort.

5. Short answers: Neither do I./I do./I don't.
(→ Unit 13.3)

	Meinung:	Zustimmung:	Widerspruch:
present simple:	I like Kathy's lounge. I do**n't** like the children's bedroom.	So do I. **Neither** do I.	I don't. I do.
past simple:	I liked the modern flat. I did**n't** like the old cottage.	So did I. **Neither** did I.	I didn't. I did.

6. Possessive pronouns (nominal form): theirs
(→ Unit 9.5/10.3/11.5)

– Here's my suitcase.
– And **your parents' luggage**?
– **Theirs** is still in the car.

Schlüssel

Unit 1

A 1
- Good evening.
- *Good* evening.
- *My* name's Frank Johnson. *What's* your name?
- My *name's* Thea Schmitt.

A 2
Sie: I'm *(Ihr Vorname und Name)* and *this* is *(Namen der Bekannten)*.
Kanadier: Good evening.
Bekannte: Good evening.
Sie: And *what's your* name?
Kanadier: I'm/My *name's* Paul Wright.

A 3
Judy: Good evening. I'm Judy Brown.
Sie: Good *evening*. My name's *(Ihr Vorname und Name)*.
Freund: And *I'm* Dieter Kühn.
Judy: I'm from New York. Where are you *from*?
Sie: I'm from *(Ihr Wohnort)*.
Freund: And I'm *from (gleicher Ort), too.*

A 4 ➔ A 5
1. Gast: Good evening. My *name's* Ellis Miller.
   Sie: Good *evening*. I'm *(Ihr Vorname und Name)*. I'm from *(Ihr Wohnort)*. This *is* Frau Nissen.
   Gast: Where's *she* from?
   Sie: She's *from* Bremen. – And *this* is Herr Kluve.
   Gast: Where's *he* from?
   Sie: He's *from* Bremen, *too*. – This *is* Frl. Braun; she's *from* Salzburg. And Herr Bertschi's *from* Berne.
2. **a** Judy Brown's from New York. **b** Frau Nissen's from Bremen. **c** Herr Kluve's from Bremen (, too). **d** Frl. Braun's from Salzburg. **e** Herr Bertschi's from Berne.

Unit 2

A 1
Alan: Hello, Richard.
Richard: Hello, Alan.
Alan: How are you?
Richard: Not so bad, thanks.
Alan: Hello, Susan.
Susan: Hello, Alan. Alan, this is Miss Jones from Leeds.
Alan: How do you do?
Miss J.: How do you do?

Mike R.: How do you do? I'm Mike Rogers.
Thomas P.: How do you do? I'm Thomas Price.
Mike R.: Nice to meet you.

A 2
a This is his *father*.
b This is *his* mother.
c And this is *his wife*.
d This is her *husband*.
e This is *her daughter*.
f And this is *her son*.

A 2 ➔ A 3
a shop-assistant; *a* housewife; *an* electrician; *a* clerk; *a* dentist; *an* engineer; *a* waitress

A 2 ➔ A 4
S.: The Jones Family: Frank Jones ...
Q.: What's his job?
S.: He's *a teacher*.
Q.: What's *his* phone number?
S.: It's 7 33 - 21 45.
And his wife Susan ...
Q.: What's *her* job?
S.: She's a teacher, too.
And his father and mother, Richard and Ann Jones.
Q.: Richard ... What's *his* job?
S.: He's an electrician.
Q.: And Ann ...
S.: She's a housewife.

A 4
It's a *house*.

A 1 ➔ B 1
a *Goodbye*. Alle anderen sind Begrüßungsformeln.
b *How do you do?* Alle anderen sind Verabschiedungsformeln.
c *husband.* Alle anderen sind weibliche Familienmitglieder.
d *daughter.* Alle anderen sind Berufsbezeichnungen.
e *Mr.* Alle anderen sind Verwandtschaftsbezeichnungen.

Schlüssel

B1 ➜ B2

Name	Job	Room	Phone
Clarke, Brenda	secretary	7	907
Francis, Ann	export manager	3	833
Harris, Simon	translator	5	905
Morrison, Alan	general manager	1	831
Müller, Thomas	assistant	4	834
Taylor, June	typist	6	906
Wilson, John	assistant manager	2	832

B3
1. **b** ist die beste Antwort.
   a und **c** wirken abrupt und unvermittelt.
2. **c** ist richtig, da es sich um eine formelle Vorstellung handelt; deshalb *How do you do?* höflich erwidern.
   a ist falsch, beantwortet die Frage *How are you?*.
   b ist unpassend, zu abrupt.
3. **c** ist eine mögliche gute Antwort.
   a Sich noch einmal in so kurzer Zeit vorzustellen ist nicht notwendig, zu steif.
   b Es ist abend (siehe 1).
4. **b** ist korrekt.
   a und **c**: Falsche Person: *They* bzw. *He* statt *I*.
5. **a** ist die beste Antwort.
   b beantwortet die Frage nicht.
   c ist nicht höflich genug.

B4
a see **b** where **c** he's **d** her **e** Joan **f** no
g Miss

Unit 3

A1
a Switzerland, Swiss **b** France, French
c Britain, British **d** Austria, Austrian
e Germany, German

A2 ➜ A3
1. **a** Yes, *they are*. **b** Yes, *they are*. **c** Excuse me, *are the* secretaries in room 3? – No, *they aren't*. They*'re* in room 4.

2. **a** *It's in* room 3. **b** *Excuse me, where's* the conversation group? – *It's in* room 7. **c** *Excuse me, where are* the beginners, *please?* – *They're in* room 1. **d** *Excuse me, where's* the business English course? – *It's in* room 5.

A1 ➜ A3
– Hello, my name's Mary Bourke.
– *Hello,* I'm Doris Schulze. And *this is* Ulrike Brand.
– Hello, Ulrike, nice *to meet you.*
  Where *are* you from?
– *We're/I'm from* Germany.
  Are you English, Mary?
– No, I'm *not*. I'm Irish!
  Are you a student, Doris?
– Yes, *I am*. And you?
– I'm *an* engineer.
– Oh, Ulrike*'s an* engineer, too.

A4 ➜ A5
– Where *do* you live?
– I *live* in Liverpool. My father and mother *live in* Dublin. And where *do you live?*
– I *live* in Kiel.
– *Does* Ulrike *live in* Kiel, too?
– No, *she lives in* Frankfurt.

A6
– Good evening, sir.
– Good evening. I'd like a room, please.
– Would you like a single room or a double room?
– We'd like a double room, please.
– Yes, sir, with a bath or a shower?
– With a shower, please.
– Yes, sir, room 10. Here's your key.
– Thank you.

A7 ➜ A8
What's *her* address?
Oh, how *do you* spell that, please?
Oh, what's *her* name, please?
Err, *how do you* spell *that?*

A8
a, j, k [eɪ]
b, c, d, e, g, p, t, v [iː]
q, u, w [uː]
y, i [aɪ]

A 9

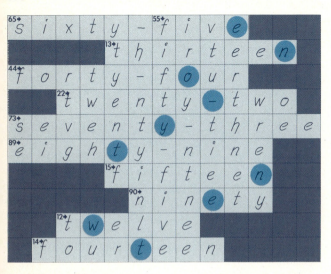

Lösungszahl: *twenty-one*

B 1
a false **b** true **c** false **d** true **e** false **f** true

B 2
a 21 p, twenty-one pence/p
b £ 7.17, seven pounds seventeen
c £ 1.55, one pound fifty-five
d £ 56.12, fifty-six pounds twelve

B 3
a Karen Hinnekint lives in Rotterdam. She's a secretary. In her free time she works in the garden.
b Renate and Uwe Petersen live in Kiel. They're dentists./She's a dentist and he's a dentist, too. In their free time they play tennis.
c Ian Thomas lives in Manchester. He's a clerk. In his free time he reads books.
d Artur Hügli lives in Berne. He's a shop-assistant. In his free time he plays football.
e Carla and Giovanni Vadini live in Rome. She's/Carla's a teacher and he's/Giovanni's an engineer. In their free time they watch television.

Unit 4

A 1 ➔ A 2
1. **a** Turn left. **b** Turn right. **c** Go straight on.
2. **a** in **b** in, near **c** at **d** near **e** in **f** into
3. **a** in, next to, opposite **b** in, near

A 3
a Turn *left* here, then turn *right* at the *second* corner and *left* at the *third* corner; the exit is then *straight on*.
b Go *straight on* and turn *right* into the *third* lane. Then *turn left at the second corner, then right, then left, and the exit is straight on*.

A 2 ➔ A 4
a – Excuse me, is there a café near here?
– I think there's one in King Street. Go straight on, turn right at the bus stop, and the café's on your right.
– Thanks.
b – Excuse me, is there a police station near here?
– Sorry, I don't know. (I'm a stranger here, too.)
c – Excuse me, is there a toilet near here?
– Yes, there's one over there on the left.
– (Oh yes,) Thank you.
d – Excuse me, is there a hotel near here?
– Yes, there's one in Market Lane. Turn left here and the Station Hotel is on your left, opposite the Odeon Cinema.
– Thanks.
e – Excuse me, is there a pub near here?
– Sorry, I don't know. (I'm a stranger here, too.)

A 5
a Metropole Hotel
– Is *this* London Bridge?
– *Yes*, *it is*.
– And what's *that* over there?
– *That's* Tower Bridge.
– Is *this* my hotel?
– No, *it isn't*. *That's* your hotel over there.

b At the pub
– Is *this* my drink?
– No, *this* is my drink. *That's* your drink.

Schlüssel

B 1

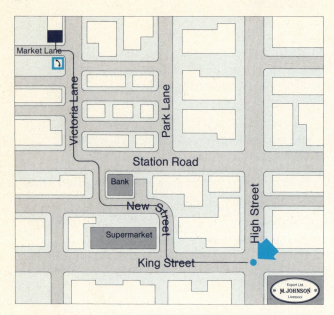

B 1 ➔ B 3

a – Excuse me, *where's* Thomas Müller, please?
   – The new assistant from Germany? *He's* in room *four*. Turn *right* and *his* office is the *third* on the left.
   – Thank you.
b – *Excuse* me, *where's* June Taylor, *please?*
   – June? *She's in* room *six*. Turn *right* and *her* office is here at the corner, the first *(room) on the right*.
   – Thanks.
c – Where's the general manager, *please?*
   – Mr Morrison? *He's in* room *one* – the *second* office on *the left*.
   – Thank you.
d – Excuse me, *where's* John Wilson, please?
   – John Wilson? *He's in* room *two*. *His* office is *straight on*, over *there*.
   – Thanks.
e – Excuse me, *where's* Ann Francis, *please?*
   – Here – I'm Ann Francis!

B 4

a true
b false. Nancy is the first daughter.
c true
d false. Susan, the second daughter, is thirteen.
e true

Unit 5

A 1 ➔ A 2

1. **a** It's *ten past eight* in *Edinburgh*. **b** It's *ten past nine* in *Nuremberg*. **c** *It's ten past three in Boston.* **d** In *Bombay* it's *twenty to two*.
2. **a** It's quarter past nine. **b** It's almost ten to seven. **c** It's 8 o'clock in New York. It's 1 o'clock in London. And it's 2 o'clock in Augsburg.
3. **a** Excuse *me, can you tell me the time,* please? **b** *Excuse me,* what's *the time, please?*

A 3 ➔ A 4

1. **a** *thirty-second, thirtieth.* **b** The *twenty-eighth* of December. Woodrow Wilson: *the twenty-eighth* US president. **c** John Quincy Adams: *the sixth* US president. *The eleventh of July.*
2. **a** The *twelfth* of February is Lincoln's birthday. Abraham Lincoln: the *sixteenth* US president. **b** The *fourteenth of February* is St Valentine's Day. **c** The *twenty-second of February* is George Washington's *birthday*. Washington: *the first* US president.
3. **a** No, it isn't. It's on the twenty-fourth (of December). **b** It's on the thirty-first of December. **c** Yes, it is.

A 5 ➔ A 6

1. – Oh, no, *I haven't*. Have *you* got your Christmas shopping list?
   – Yes, I have. And *have you got* our map of London?
   – No, I haven't. Have you got the address of the tea shop?
   – Yes, I have. Have you got Jenny's phone number?
   – Yes, I have.
2. i. **b** ist die sprachlich korrekte und höfliche Antwort. **a** wäre unhöflich. **c** sagt man, wenn man etwas Angebotenes annimmt.
   ii. **c** ist allein angemessen, weil höfliches Bedauern gezeigt wird. **a** wirkt kurz angebunden, **b** unhöflich.
   iii. **c** ist die einzige inhaltlich stimmige Antwort. **a** und **b** wären Antworten auf die Frage *How are you?*.

A 7

1. The North Devon Tour takes about 12 hours from Birmingham. The coach *leaves Birmingham at 8.15 on Mondays*. It *returns to Birmingham at 8.45 in the evening*. The *North Devon Tour is £6.40 per person*.

Schlüssel

2. The Snowdonia Tour *takes about 11 hours from Birmingham. The coach leaves Birmingham at 9.25 on Wednesdays. It returns to Birmingham at 9 o'clock in the evening. The Snowdonia Tour is £5.00 per person.*
3. The Hadrian's Wall Tour *takes about 14 hours from Birmingham. The coach leaves Birmingham at 8.10 on Mondays and Fridays. It returns to Birmingham at 10.45 in the evening. The Hadrian's Wall Tour is £6.35 per person.*

B 1 ➜ B 2
zu B 1: **a** false – July *12th* **b** true **c** false – at 5.30 and *8.30* **d** true **e** false – £4.00, £2.50 and £1.50
zu B 2: **a** false – The *fourteenth* Cambridge Folk Festival **b** true **c** false – at 6.15 *p.m.*
d false – on the *30th/thirtieth* **e** true
f false – At half past *nine.* **g** false – *Six pounds.*

B 1 ➜ B 3
1. **a** Here's Susan! **b** Is he English? **c** They're free.
d Hello, Ellen.
2. **a** Mr Lennard's over there. **b** It's the third street on the left. **c** I'm in room 30. **d** E – L – S – A.
[iː – eI – es – eI]
3. **a** On the thirtieth of July, Diz Disley's on.
b Tickets are available on Monday and Tuesday.
c The Ford Cortina costs £70 for five days.
d No, I'm sorry, we haven't. But we've got a Mini.

Unit 6

A 1 ➜ A 3
1. **a** ist die beste Antwort.
b *What time?* fragt nach dem Zeitpunkt; üblicher wäre es, zuerst den Zeitraum (Tag) festzulegen. Dazu dient in **a** die Frage *When?*
c *That's fine.* sagt man erst, wenn etwas abgemacht ist.
2. **c** ist die beste Antwort.
a und **b** wirken unhöflich, weil für die Absage kein Grund gegeben wird.
3. **b** ist die richtige Antwort. Es wird um eine nähere Angabe (Zeitpunkt) gebeten.
a wie bei 2: zu kurz, um höflich zu sein.
c *I'd love to.* haben Sie schon bei 1 gesagt; es sollte nicht wiederholt werden.

4. **b** ist die richtige Antwort.
a sagt man nur bei der Vorstellung.
c paßt nicht zur Ankündigung des Engländers.
5. **b** ist die richtige Antwort.
a wäre die Antwort auf die Frage *Are you doing anything this evening?*
c wäre die Antwort auf eine direkte Einladung/einen bestimmten Vorschlag.
6. **a** ist die richtige Antwort.
b und **c** beantworten die Frage nicht.

A 4
– Why *can't* John *come?*
– Because he's *playing football./going to a football match.*
– And why *can't* Liz *come?*
– Because *she's working* on Saturday evening.
– And why *can't* Thomas *come?*
– Because *he's going to Canterbury* for the weekend.
– Why *can't* Graham and Susan *come?*
– Because *they're going to the theatre.*

A 1 ➜ A 5
a Mary *reads books.* **b** The Morrisons *read magazines.*
c Tom *works in the garden.* **d** Robert *goes to the theatre.*

A 5 ➜ A 6
a unter Fremden **b** unter Fremden **c** bei Bekannten
d unter Fremden **e** bei Bekannten
Die Situation 'unter Fremden' ist relativ formell. Sprachliche Merkmale der passenden höflichen Redeweise sind z. B.:
– die Einleitung einer Frage mit *Excuse me …;*
– die längeren Formulierungen: *Would you like … ?, Thank you., It's not allowed.;*
– die Erwiderung mit *That's OK.* auf *Thank you.*
Merkmale des informelleren Stils, 'unter Bekannten', sind u. a.:
– *Excuse me …* als Einleitung kann weggelassen werden;
– kürzere umgangssprachliche Formulierungen wie *Thanks., Yes, sure.,* usw.;
– auf *Thanks.* erwidert man meist nichts.

Schlüssel

B 1

B 2

1. Die Reihenfolge der Bilder ist Nr. 2, 4, 3, 1.
2. Thanks for the photos and the invitation to visit you. *I'd love to* come, but I'm sorry, *I can't* because *I'm working* this summer. *I've got* a summer job from July till September: an English firm here needs a German typist.
What do *I do* in my free time? *I play* tennis. And *I watch* the English and American films on our "third programme" on TV. Are there German films on British television?

B 3

a true – ergibt sich aus Joes Telefonnummer: Manchester 4 77 66. **b** false. Friday is/It's Joe's birthday. **c** true **d** false. Joan/She can't come to the party. **e** false. They're coming on the 18th. **f** false. Her friends are/They're Austrian. **g** true. **h** true.

B 4
a, an, at, I, in, is, it, into, no, not, so, son, station, to

Unit 7

A 1
1–7–5; 2–11–6; 1–9–4; 2–8–3–4; 2–10–3–5

A 1 ➜ A 3
a shirt **b** coat **c** shirt **d** shorts **e** sandals **f** blouse **g** jeans **h** shoes **i** pullover **j** jeans **k** sandals/shoes **l** shirt **m** dress **n** trousers

A 2 ➜ A 4
a *larger* **b** *smaller* **c** A British size 15½ is *too small* for you. You need a *larger* one. **d** *larger* **e** so it's too *expensive* for you. You need *a cheaper* one. **f** That's about *DM 35,–* ... so it's *cheaper* than in Britain.

A 4 ➜ A 5
a Austria is *larger than* Switzerland. **b** 'Betty Crocker's Cookbook' is *more expensive than* 'The Vegetarian Cookbook'. **c** An Austin Metro *is cheaper than a* Ford Cortina. **d** A day *is shorter than 1450 minutes*. **e** The trousers *are shorter than* the jeans. **f** Many Germans think German beer *is better than* British/English beer. **g** The centre of Frankfurt *is more modern than* the centre of Heidelberg. **h** Many people think the TV *is more interesting than books, the theatre and concerts*.

B 1
a Yes, they do. **b** Yes, you/I can. **c** It's £18.95. **d** The woman's coat is more expensive. It costs £29. **e** The boy's anorak is cheaper. **f** Yes, they do. **g** They are £5.75. **h** No, they aren't, they are more expensive.

B 2
1. **a, f** 2. **e, f** 3. **b** 4. **c, d** 5. **b, c** 6. **a, f**

B 3
1.

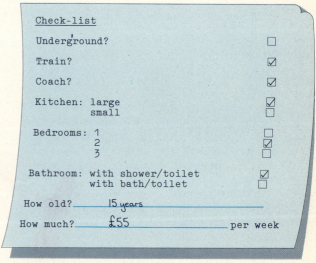

2. **a** false **b** true **c** false **d** true **e** true **f** false **g** false **h** true **i** false **j** false

Schlüssel

Unit 8

A1 → A2

1. **a** No, she wasn't, because she was at the office till seven (o'clock). **b** Yes, she was. **c** No, she wasn't, because she was so/too/very tired. **d** She was at the folk club. **e** Perhaps they were at John's place.
2. "Yes, I *was* at the office till seven yesterday. Then I *had* a pizza at an Italian restaurant, and after that I *had* three coffees because I *was* so tired.
Where *were* you last night? –
Oh, you *were* at the folk club! *Was* it good? –
So you *had* a great time yesterday. *Were* John and his friends at the club, too? –
Oh, perhaps they *were* at John's place then. –
OK, see you at the club on Saturday evening. Bye!"

A3 → A4

a No, I didn't. I watched 'The Kid' on BBC 2.
b No, I didn't. I was at the office till nine.
c Yes, I was. I/We had a club meeting on Friday evening.
d No, I didn't. I wanted to watch the/a football match on TV.
e Yes, I was/we were. I/We had guests from Switzerland.

A5 → A7

a *When* was he born?
b *Where* did he go to school and university?
c *What* did he do in 1920?
d *Where* did he make 'The 39 Steps'?
e *Why* did Hitchcock leave Britain?
f *What* film did he make in 1960?
g *When* did Elizabeth II make Hitchcock 'Sir Alfred'?
h *Where* did Hitchcock die?

B1
1. **d** 2. **c** 3. **b** 4. **d** 5. **c** 6. **d** 7. **c** 8. **c**

B2 → B3
A group of people from Gloucester *visited* their twin city Trier and *wanted* to go to the Trier museum. Their hosts *wanted* to take them, but the English visitors *said*: "We can find our way."
About an hour later, the visitors *phoned* their hosts. "Where are you?", the hosts *asked*.
"We don't really know," *was* the answer, "but the name of the street is 'Einbahnstraße'!"

B1 → B3
had, watched, did, wanted, played, flew – *are*
went, signed, met, married, lived, died – *you*
left, enjoyed, travelled, invited, attended, started – *a*
visited, made, resulted, said, stayed – *beginner*
Lösungssatz: *Are you a beginner?*

Unit 9

A1 → A2
In a department store: 1. **d** 2. **b**
Booking a room: 1. **c** 2. **a**
Reserving a table: 1. **c** 2. **d**

In a department store
1. Excuse me, where can I find postcards?
2. Can I get stamps there, too?

Booking a room
1. Can I reserve a single room for next week?
2. Can you spell 'Maier', please?

Reserving a table
1. Can I reserve a table for this evening?
2. Can I have your name, please?

A3
a Waiter, can you bring me a knife, please?
b Waiter, can you bring me a spoon, please?
c ... a fork ... **d** ... a glass and the pepper ...
e ... a glass and a plate ... **f** ... the salt and pepper, and a plate ...
Alternativantworten: Waiter, can I have a knife, please? etc.

A4

	Ann:	Jill:
To start with:	chicken soup	tomato juice
To follow:	lamb chops	the same
To drink:	tea	red wine

A5 → A6
1. ... the weather here's *cold/(and) wet* ...... my bed's so *uncomfortable* ... the food here's *(too/very) expensive/not very nice.* The other guests are *not very interesting/not very nice* ... the sea's *too cold.*

Schlüssel

one hundred and forty-four 144

2. Es passen in allen Lücken (außer der zweiten): *nice/very nice;* sonst auch: ... Jersey's *great* ... the weather's not so *cold/(and) wet* ... It's *(very) comfortable/not very expensive* ... the summer guests here are *interesting* ... a *great* little pub.

A 7 ➜ A 8
a No, it doesn't. (You need the 36.)
b You need the 32./Take the 32.
c Yes, it does.
d (I think you have to) take the 36./You need the 36.
e (I think you have to) take the 35./You need the 35.
f (I think you have to) take the 34./You need the 34.

B 1

Reimwörter	Reimlaut	Es reimt sich nicht:
a soup group	[uːp]	hope [həʊp] cup [kʌp] couple [ˈkʌpl]
b steak take	[eɪk]	week [wiːk] speak [spiːk] like [laɪk]
c peas cheese please	[iːz]	police [pəˈliːs]
d pie fly I goodbye buy	[aɪ]	tea [tiː] free [friː]
e toast post	[əʊst]	—
f four more or door	[ɔː]	hour [ˈaʊə]
g two you through do	[uː]	go [gəʊ] now [naʊ]

B 2
a Mike b Mike c Mary d Mary *and* Mike

B 3 ➜ B 4
a *Claremont Hotel* (because it's got a New Year Party)
b *Waldorf Hotel* (because children and dogs are welcome)

B 4
I *saw* your advertisement *in* the newspaper this morning. I'd like to *reserve* accommodation *for* three persons (I've *got* two children, ages 5 and 3) *from* Saturday, July 4th *to* Saturday, July 18th. I'd *like* a flat with 2 single beds for the children.
I *enclose* a deposit of £9.

Unit 10

A 1
a "We want to go shopping."
b "I want to have a tour of the city."
c "I'd like to have a tour of the city, too."
d "We'd like to visit our/some American friends."
e "I want to rent a car and drive to New York City."

A 2
a – I'm sorry. I didn't see that.
b – I'm sorry. I'm not used to English money yet.
  – That's all right.
c – I'm sorry. I didn't see that.
  – That's all right.

A 3
– Sorry, I *didn't quite understand.* ...
– *No, I'm sorry,* we don't ...
– Oh, err, can *you repeat that, please?*

A 4 ➜ A 5
1. a shortest b most difficult c most expensive
   d hottest e smallest f newest
2. – Well, it's the *cheapest* car and the *easiest* car to park ...
   – Well, yes, but. ... I'd prefer a Rover. It's the *largest.*
   – But Geoff, it's in the *most expensive* group!

A 6
1. a Oh, let's take a Vauxhalle Chevette.
     Oh, shall we take a Vauxhalle Chevette?
   b Well, let's take a Chrysler Sunbeam.
     Well, shall we take a Chrysler Sunbeam?
2. Alice: "*Let's take* a Vauxhall Chevette."
   Geoff: "*I'd prefer* a Rover."

Schlüssel

A 7
1. **a** English **b** Spanish **c** Russian **d** German
   e French **f** Italian
2. **a** They speak Dutch.
   b It comes from the USA.
      They/The Americans speak English.
   c It comes from Zurich. – Yes, they do.
   d It comes from Austria.
      Most people there speak German.
   e They understand Russian.
   f Yes, it does. – Yes, I do./Yes, I speak it fluently.

B 1
a true **b** true **c** true **d** false

B 2
a Brian *1*, Ann *4*, David *5*, Ellen *8*, Mrs Johnson *6*, Mr Johnson *7*
b Brian: Shall we go for a swim on Sunday?
  Ann: Let's play tennis instead.
  David: I want to sleep till twelve o'clock!
  Ellen: I want to write some letters.
  Mrs J.: I'd prefer to go for a walk.
  Mr J.: I'd like a good meal.
c 5, 6, 7

Unit 11

A 1 ➔ A 2
Die Dominosteine können wie folgt zusammengesetzt werden: 1–2–3–6–9; 1–2–5–10–4–8; 1–5–4–8–10; 1–5–10–4–8; 1–6–3–7–9

A 3
a Don't eat too many eggs. **b** Don't smoke too many cigars. **c** Don't drink too much cola. **d** Don't drink too much cognac. **e** Don't use too much salt.
f Don't eat too much ice-cream.

A 4
1. **a** ist die beste Antwort.
   b *What time?* fragt nach dem Zeitpunkt; üblicher wäre es, zuerst den Zeitraum (Tag) festzulegen. Dazu dient die Frage *When?*.
   c drückt Zustimmung aus, wenn etwas abgemacht wird.
2. **c** ist die beste Antwort.
   a und **b** wirken unhöflich, weil für die Absage kein Grund gegeben wird.
3. **b** ist die beste Antwort.
   a und **c** sind Erwiderungen im anderen Zusammenhang, nämlich zu: *I'm much better ...* bzw. *How are you?*.
4. **a** ist die beste Antwort.
   b wird eher als Antwort auf Vorschläge wie *Let's/Shall we ...?* verwendet.
   c wird nur zur Bestätigung verwendet; z. B. *Oh, you're Swiss. – Yes, that's right.*
5. **b** ist die richtige Antwort.
   b sagt man nur bei der Vorstellung (vgl. U 2/A 1).
   c paßt nicht zur Ankündigung des Engländers.

A 4 ➔ A 5
Tuesday: *hairdresser's,* Wednesday: *German class,* Thursday: *theatre group,* Friday: *shopping with Ann*

A 6
a – Excuse me, that's my *hat*.
   – Oh, I'm sorry. I thought it was *mine*.
b – Excuse me, those are my *gloves*.
   – Oh, I'm sorry. I thought they were *mine*.
c – Excuse me, that isn't *yours*.
   – Oh, I'm sorry. I though it was my *(rain)coat*.
d – Excuse me, those aren't *yours*.
   – Oh, I'm sorry. I thought they were my *suitcases*.
e – Excuse me, that's my *bag*.
   – Oh, I'm sorry. I thought it was *mine*.
f – Excuse me, that isn't *yours*.
   – Oh, I'm sorry. I thought it was my *(over)coat*.

B 1 ➔ B 2
1. **b** ist die beste Antwort.
   a und **c** wirken zu abrupt und deshalb unhöflich.
2. **b** ist die beste Antwort.
   a und **c**, da sie keine Erklärung beifügen, wirken unhöflich.
3. **c** ist richtig. **a** und **b** sind unzutreffend.
4. **a** ist richtig. **b** ist falsch. **c** paßt nur zu einer gesellschaftlichen Einladung.

B 4
The south of England and South Wales *will be* sunny and *hot* ...
London and the Midlands *will* also *be* dry and *sunny* ...
There *will be* sunny periods in North Wales ..., and it *will be* generally *very warm* ...
The north of Scotland ... *will have* ... a little *rain* ...
It *will be* much cooler on the coasts with *fog* in the east.

Schlüssel

B1 ➔ B5

¹A	P	²P	³O	⁴I	N	T	M	E	N	⁵T

(Crossword solution:)
1. APPOINTMENT
2. POET
3. OUT
4. MENU
5. TELL
6. RAIN
7. NIL
8. PHONE
9. COLDS
10. DRY (DS/DR)
11. TOOTH
12. ON
13. STOMACH-ACHE

(Down words include: AMERICAN, POET, OUT/OTT, MENU/UNC, TELEPHONE, NIL, DRY, ON)

Unit 12

A1 ➔ A2
Die Reihenfolge der Bilder ist:
a ③   b ② ①
  ① ④   ④
  ⑤ ②   ③

A2 ➔ A3
– Can you help me, please?
– What's wrong?
– (I think) There's something wrong with the engine.
– OK, I'll have a look.

A4
– No, *I haven't* … Have you *closed* all the *windows*?
– Yes, *I have.*
– *Have you turned off* the *heating*?
– Yes, and I've *turned off the radio,* too.
– Oh, good. And have *you checked the tyres?*
– Yes, *I have* …

A5
a There's some (beer) left. They don't need any.
b There's some (gin) left. They don't need any.
c There isn't any (tonic water) left. They'll have to buy/get some.
d There are some (paper plates) left. They don't need any.
e There's some (orange juice) left. They don't need any.
f There aren't any (crisps) left. They'll have to buy/get some.
g There aren't any (peanuts) left. They'll have to buy/get some.

A6
1. a Yes, she has. b No, not yet./No, she hasn't. c No, she isn't. d Yes, she is. e No, not yet./she hasn't. f Yes, she can.
2. a false. She wants to have a party on Saturday. b false. She hasn't bought anything to eat and drink yet. c false. She's going to invite some colleagues. d true

A7
a – Would you like *a cigarette*?
 – Yes, I'd love one.
b – Would you like some *wine*?
 – No, thank you. I've *just had some.*
c – Would you like *a cup of tea*?
 – Yes, *I'd love one.*
d – Would you like an *orange juice*?
 – No, thank you. *I've just hand one.*
e – Would you like *a sandwich*?
 – No, *thank you. I've just had one.*
f – Would you like some *crisps*?
 – Yes, I'd love *some.*
g – Would you like *a beer*?
 – Yes, I'd love one.
h – Would you like *a gin and tonic*?
 – No, *thank you. I've just had* one.

A8
1. **b**   2. **c**   3. **a** oder **d**

B1
– Hello, this is John Smith in room 22. I think there's something *wrong* with my shower. Can you come and *check* it, please?
– Certainly, sir. I'll *tell* our assistant manager. He'll *come* up to your room right away. – Can I help you with *anything* else?

– You've got *trouble* with your shower, sir?
– Yes. There isn't *any* water.
– Oh, I'll have a *look*. Hmm. Yes, there's *something* wrong with it. I'm afraid we can't *repair* it at the moment. I'm terribly *sorry*, but you'll *have to* take *another* room.

B 2 ➔ B 3
1. **a**   2. **b**   3. **c**   4. **b**

B 1 ➔ B 4
1. **b**   2. **b**   3. **a**   4. **a**   5. **a**   6. **b**   7. **a**

Unit 13

A 1 ➔ A 2
a true   **b** true   **c** false. They went last Saturday.
d true   **e** false   **f** true   **g** false. The raincoat at Evans's was too small.   **h** true

A 3
was quite good = *wasn't bad;* was excellent = *was very good;* was very nice = *was very good;* wasn't very good = *wasn't very nice*

A 3 ➔ A 4
a – Yes sure, I *flew* to Chicago …
– Well, I've never *flown* …
– No, I've never *seen/visited* Edinburgh …
– So you haven't …
– No, I *haven't.* I've never *visited* any castles.
– And have you ever …?
– Yes, I *have.* David and I *went* on a pub tour in London …
– Have you ever *been* on a tour of the Highlands?
– No, I *haven't.*
b – And what *was* the tour of the city like?
– It *was* very interesting. And I *bought* a lot of souvenirs on the way.
– Was the theatre good?
– Yes, it *was* excellent.
– What *was* Edinburgh Castle *like?*
– Oh, I liked it …
– And what *was* the pub tour *like?*
– We haven't *been on* the pub tour yet … By the way, have you got my postcard yet? I *sent* it yesterday.
– No, I haven't …

A 5
Folgende Wörter sollten durchgestrichen werden:
a smallest   **b** most difficult   **c** most comfortable
d easiest   **e** most unsuccessful   **f** happiest

A 6
Sinnvolle Gespräche sind:
1 – 2 – 4
1 – 3 – 5 – 8 – 9
1 – 3 – 6 – 7 – 9
1 – 3 – 6 – 7 – 8 – 9

B 1
1. **a** false   **b** true   **c** false   **d** false   **e** false   **f** true   **g** true
2. **a** I was born in … on …   **b** I went to school in … from … to/till …   **c** I left school in …   **d** I was/am a/an …   **e** Yes, I did/do. – No, I didn't/don't.   **f** I'm a/an …   **g** (wie **e**)

B 3
a true   **b** true   **c** false. Fred prefered (drank) Coke.
d false. They often tried to slim.   **e** true   **f** false. It's the cheapest way to slim.   **g** false. It doesn't have to be dull.

B 1 ➔ B 3

a
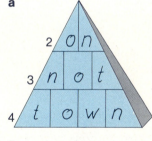

b
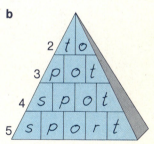

c
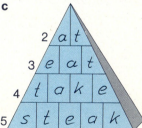

Schlüssel

Unit 14

A1 → A2
a true b false. It was quite near (it). c true d false. She didn't like it because it was on a busy main road. e false. The cottage (It) is really cheap. f false. They liked it immediately. g true h false. Kathy (and the children) was (were) so enthusiastic that Peter finally agreed. i false. They have to renovate the cottage completely. j true

A3
It's going to rain on someone/on the man.

A2 + A4
1. **b** ist richtig. **a** und **c** sind falsch, da die Frage mit *have* gebildet ist.
2. **a** ist richtig. **b** ist falsch (wie Nr. 1). **c** paßt nicht zur Frage.
3. **b** ist richtig. **a** und **c** sind falsch, da sie Reaktionen auf positive Aussagen sind. **a** ist außerdem past simple, also falsche Zeit.

A5
a – No they aren't *mine*. Perhaps they're *theirs*.
b – ... are these *your* keys?
   – No, they aren't *ours/mine*.
c – Oh, *my* keys!

A6
Reihenfolge der Bilder (von links nach rechts):
5, 3,
4, 1, 2

A7
a Between the toilets (WC) and the boating lake (4).
b At/In the farm shop.

B1 → B2
Linda: 2, 4 (Not 1, 5, 8 because she has never worked in an office and can't type.)
Sally: 3 (She doesn't want office or part-time work.)

B3

Lösung: ON THE WAY

Hörtexte

Unit 3

B 1
- Hello, I'm Jacques Delon.
- Hello, my name's Anna Bessoni. – Are you French?
- Yes, I am. I live in Paris. – And you? Are you Italian?
- No, I'm not. I'm Swiss.
- Where do you live in Switzerland?
- In Lugano. – What's your job, Jacques?
- I'm a teacher.
- Oh – are you in the advanced group?
- No, I'm not an *English* teacher! I'm on the refresher course. – And you?
- I'm in the English for Secretaries group.
- Oh, you're a secretary.
- Yes, that's right.

Unit 4

B 1
- Well, you go down King Street, turn right into New Street ...
- At the supermarket?
- Yes, there's a supermarket on the corner. Go straight on ...
- Into New Street?
- Yes. Go down New Street and turn right at the bank. That's the first – no, the second street on the right.
- The second street on the right – yes.
- Then turn right into Station Road and ... No, no, turn *left* into Station Road and the first street on the right is Victoria Lane.
- Victoria Lane – yes.
- Yes. Go down Victoria Lane and I live in the third street on the left – Market Lane – on the corner opposite the phone-box.
- OK. See you later, then.

Unit 5

A 1 ➔ A 2
2. **a** – Excuse me, can you tell me the time, please?
   – It's quarter past nine.
   – Thank you very much.
b – Excuse me, what's the time, please?
   – Err ..., it's almost ten to seven.
   – Thank you.
c In New York it's 8 o'clock now. It's 1 o'clock in London and 2 o'clock in Augsburg.

Unit 6

A 5 ➔ A 6
- Hello.
- Hello, John! What about a drink?

- Excuse me, can I smoke here?
- No, I'm afraid you can't. It's not allowed.

- Can I smoke here?
- Yes, of course.
- Would you like a cigarette?
- No, thank you. I smoke cigarillos.

- Can I smoke here?
- Yes, sure. Have you got a cigarette for me, too?
- Yes. Here you are.

- Excuse me, can I borrow your map, please?
- Yes, of course.
- Thank you.
- That's OK.

- Peter, can I see your newspaper, please?
- Yes, sure.
- Thanks.

B 3
- Manchester 47766.
- Hello, Joe. This is Joan.
- Hello, Joan. How are you?
- Not so bad, thanks. And you?
- OK. – Are you coming to my birthday party on Friday?
- I'd love to – thanks for your invitation – but I'm sorry, I can't. Some friends from Austria are visiting me at the weekend. They're coming on the eighteenth.
- Well, would you like to bring them with you?
- I'm afraid not. They only speak German.
- Oh. – Can you speak German?!
- Of course. Can't you?
- Ha ha. – Well, see you Monday at our evening class then.
- OK. See you then. Bye.
- Bye.

Hörtexte

Unit 7

B 3

Well, the flat's in 72 Park Lane, 60 minutes from the city centre by train, 80 minutes by coach. There's a coach stop in Park Lane, and the railway station isn't very far from the flat.
The flat's got a large kitchen, a living-room with a TV, a balcony ... err ... it's got two bedrooms, a bathroom with shower and toilet and an extra toilet.
It's only 15 years old and costs £ 55 per week ...

Unit 8

A 1 ➔ A 2

Yes, I was at the office till seven yesterday. Then I had a pizza at an Italian restaurant, and after that I had three coffees because I was so tired. Where were *you* last night? –
Oh, you were at the folk club! Was it good? –
So you had a great time yesterday. Were John and his friends at the club, too? –
Oh, perhaps they were at John's place then. –
OK, see you at the club on Saturday evening. Bye!

B 1

– Hello, my name's Chris Mayman.
– Hi, I'm Renate Hauser.
– Are you German?
– No, I'm Swiss. – I'm on my way back to Zurich after 4 weeks in England and Scotland. – Are you English?
– Yes, I am. I'm from Manchester. – Were you in Britain on business?
– No, I was on holiday.
– Did you have a good time?
– Oh yes, it was great!
– Where did you go?
– Well, first I stayed in London for about a week ...
– What did you do there?
– Oh, I went to theatres, concerts and a lot of pubs.
– I see! – Where did you go from London?
– Well, I rented a Mini and travelled to Oxford to visit friends.
– How did you like Oxford?
– I loved it!
– And then?
– Well, then I went to Edinburgh and from there to the Scottish Highlands. – But what about you? Are you going to Zurich on business or for a holiday?
– On business – I work for an export firm ...

B 2 ➔ B 3

A group of people from Gloucester visited their twin city Trier and wanted to go to the Trier museum. Their hosts wanted to take them, but the English visitors said: "We can find our way."
About an hour later, the visitors phoned their hosts. "Where are you?", the hosts asked.
"We don't really know," was the answer, "but the name of the street is 'Einbahnstraße'!"

Unit 9

A 1 ➔ A 2
In a department store

– Excuse me, where can I find postcards?
– Over there on the right, next to the books.
– Can I get stamps there, too?
– No. You can get stamps at the post office; there's one in Bond Street.
– Thank you.

Booking a room

– Metropole Hotel. Good evening.
– Good evening. Can I reserve a single room for next week?
– Yes, certainly, madam.
– Good. That's from Monday the 9th to Friday the 13th.
– With a bath or a shower, madam?
– Just a shower, please.
– Yes. What's your name, please?
– Maria Maier.
– Can you spell 'Maier', please?
– M-A-I-E-R.
– Thank you, madam.
– Thank you. Goodbye.
– Goodbye.

Reserving a table

– Murrays Restaurant. Good morning.
– Good morning. – Can I reserve a table for this evening?
– Yes, sir. For how many?
– For eight.
– And what time, please?
– Half past seven.
– Can I have your name, please?
– Morris.
– Thank you, sir.
– Thank you. Goodbye.
– Goodbye.

Hörtexte

Unit 10

B 2

Brian:	Shall we go for a swim on Sunday, Mum?
Mrs Johnson:	Oh, I think it's too cold for a swim, Brian.
Ann:	But it's not too cold to play tennis. Let's play tennis instead.
Mr Johnson:	But, Ann, only four people can play tennis, and there are six of us.
David:	I want to sleep till 12 o'clock!
Mrs Johnson:	You can sleep all day Saturday, David.
Ellen:	And I want to write some letters.
Ann:	Oh, that's not very interesting!
Mrs Johnson:	Well, I'd prefer to go for a walk.
Mr Johnson:	I'd like a good meal!
Ann:	Then let's sleep late – till about 10.30 –, have a big breakfast, then go for a long walk and stop for an ice-cream or a cup of coffee on the way home. OK?
Brian:	OK!
Mr Johnson:	That's a good idea, Ann.

Brian:	Shall we go for a swim on Sunday?
Ann:	Let's play tennis instead.
David:	I want to sleep till 12 o'clock.
Ellen:	I want to write some letters.
Mrs Johnson:	I'd prefer to go for a walk.
Mr Johnson:	I'd like a good meal!

Ann:	Then let's sleep late – till about 10.30 –, have a big breakfast, then go for a long walk and stop for an ice-cream or a cup of coffee on the way home. OK?

Unit 11

A 4 ➔ A 5

– Hello, Jill.
– Hello, Sally, how are you?
– Oh fine, thanks. I wanted to invite you to tea one afternoon this week. Would you like to come?
– Yes, I'd love to. When?
– Will Friday be all right?
– Well ... just a minute. I'll have a look at my diary ... Oh, no, I'm sorry, I'm going shopping with Ann on Friday.
– Are you doing anything on Thursday?
– Yes, I go to my theatre group on Thursdays.
– Oh, I see. I tried to phone you last Thursday, but of course you weren't at home. Well, will you be free on Wednesday then?
– No, I'm sorry. I go to my German class on Wednesday afternoons.
– Oh, dear. Then what about Tuesday?
– Tuesday, that's tomorrow ... Oh, I'm afraid I can't come tomorrow; I'll be at the hairdresser's. What about next week? I'll be free next Tuesday.
– OK. Will 4 o'clock on Tuesday be all right?
– Fine. See you then.
– OK. See you next week. Bye.
– Bye.

B 1 ➔ B 2

1. – Dr. Brown's surgery. Good afternoon.
2. – I'm afraid it'll be difficult today. Can you come on Friday?
3. – Hmm. What's the matter?
4. – I see. Well, can you come round at 5.30?

– Dr. Brown's surgery. Good afternoon.
– Good afternoon. I'd like to make an appointment to see the doctor.
– I'm afraid it'll be difficult today. Can you come on Friday?
– Oh, but I have to see him. I'm very ill.
– Hmm. What's the matter?
– I've got stomach-ache and a terrible headache.
– I see. Well, can you come round at 5.30?
– Yes, that'll be fine.
– What's the name, please?
– Taylor.
– Thank you. Goodbye, Mr Taylor.
– Goodbye.

Hörtexte

Unit 12

A1 ➜ A2
At the petrol station
- What do I have to do?
- Well, first you have to select the correct grade – 2, 3 or 4-star petrol. Then you remove the nozzle from the pump, place the nozzle in the petrol tank and fill as required. Finally, you replace the nozzle in the pump and pay at the cash-desk.

At the Underground station
- Excuse me, can you help me, please? I want to get to Victoria Station. What do I have to do? – How do I get there?
- First you have to buy a ticket. You can get one over there. Then you have to find your train; take the Piccadilly Line to Green Park and …
- Green Park …
- Yes, and change to the Victoria Line. Victoria Station's the first stop after Green Park.
- Thank you.

Unit 13

A1 ➜ A2
- Shrewsbury 51422.
- Hello, Liz.
- Oh, hello, Jean. How are you?
- Not so bad, thanks, just tired. I've been to the sales in town. Have you been yet?
- Oh, yes. I went with David last Saturday.
- And did you buy anything?
- Yes, we did. You know it's Janet's birthday next Saturday. She'll be nine. We bought her a pair of white jeans and a blouse. And we also bought some shirts for David.
- And for the baby?
- We didn't find anything for him. And I wanted a raincoat. I saw a nice one at Evans's – it was cheap, too – but it was too small. What about you – did you buy anything?
- Yes, a skirt, blue and yellow. I like it very much.
- Fine. Well, will I see you on Friday at the parent-teachers' meeting?
- Yes, I'll be there.
- OK, see you then. Bye.
- Bye.

Unit 14

A 7
Attention, please, ladies and gentlemen: We've just found a little boy and he wants to find his parents. We don't know his name, but he's about 3 years old. He's got jeans and a red T-shirt on. We found him not far from the restaurant, between the toilets and the boating lake, going to the farm shop.
Will the parents of this little boy please come to the farm shop to get him? The farm shop's next to the restaurant and in front of the garden centre.
Thank you.
I repeat … we've …